ALL THE WAY
HOME

AN ANTHOLOGY

30 YEARS OF ROCK TRUST

First published by Taproot Press 2022

ISBN: 978-1-8380800-5-1

The authors' right to be identified as authors of this book under the Copyright, Designs and Patents Act 1988 has been asserted.

Printed and bound by
ImprintDigital, Devon

Typeset by
Main Point Books, Edinburgh

Cover
Mark Mechan, Red Axe Design

CONTENTS

for all the young people in Scotland
with nowhere to call home tonight

Foreword

I had been CEO at Rock Trust for a few weeks when the annual Sponsored Sleepout came around and I joined the team to help as a steward. We welcomed, entertained and fed our community supporters before they got into their sleeping bags on George Street, and I stood with colleagues and volunteers to ensure that they were safe. We chatted through the night. It was great getting to know them and hearing the pride in their voices as they told passers-by about what we were doing and what their role was in Rock Trust. Every so often we would have to encourage someone who had over-indulged on their night out to keep walking so they wouldn't wake the young people, parents and teachers who were being sponsored to sleep. But after the drinkers were gone and the street cleaners came out, the smell and the noises brought my own experience as a teenager sleeping rough flooding back, and I had to walk around the corner to compose myself.

While it was my own struggles with homelessness which had first provided me with the purpose and drive to pursue this career, I rarely think back to how the experience actually felt. Instead, I have spent years hearing other young people's stories, supporting them to build and achieve their goals and aspirations, and working to challenge the systems that fail to protect them. I feel privileged to have been able to do for others what someone once did for me, but angry that young people are still experiencing what I experienced. To know that we are making a difference provides a comfort.

This collection of stories, poems, opinions, experiences and reflections marks Rock Trust's 30th year, and while we are proud of what we have achieved so far, there is still some way to go to ensure that all young people in Scotland can find a way home.

Kate Polson, Rock Trust CEO

Kate Polson (second from right), CEO of Rock Trust, with three volunteers as they prepare for the 2018 Sponsored Sleep Out.

Volunteers get settled down for a long night ahead on one of Rock Trust's annual Sponsored Sleep Outs.

Introduction

VAL McDERMID

I want Rock Trust to shut down. This is an anniversary we should not have to celebrate, because it's an admission of failure.

In spite of the best efforts of everyone involved – and I'm not suggesting for a moment that Rock Trust doesn't make an enormous positive impact – things have got worse. There are more young homeless people now than when Rock Trust started its commitment to help young people out of homelessness. The economic geographer Danny Dorling has said, 'You could argue that the census form should start to ask: 'Have you ever been homeless, and, if so, when and for how long?'

We talk a lot about social justice here in Scotland. We pride ourselves on championing a more equal society than in other parts of the UK. But when it comes to homelessness, there's no hiding place from our failure.

If we classified homelessness as an illness – because it's like an illness, in terms of the devastation it causes in the lives of those who suffer from it – there would be a public outcry. It would be vying with COVID-19 for the lead story on the news. Headlines every day – 'Still No Cure For Killer Disease'.

If homelessness were an illness, we'd be demanding a cure, never mind a vaccine. We'd be holding politicians' feet to the fire on a daily basis.

Instead, recently, nearly 30,000 Scottish households were classified as homeless. That translates to 80 households losing their homes every single day. Those households contained more than 14,000 children. That's an average of 38 children losing their homes every single day. Imagine a disease that caused serious chronic damage to a whole primary school class every single day. How could we bear that?

For most people it's a problem that's easy to ignore. It's easy to dismiss people living on the pavements begging or busking badly. They're not like us. They're junkies or jakies. They're the ones that have failed, not us. And that lets us off the hook. That excuses us from looking beyond the obvious.

And that's where we fail. Because the rough sleepers we pass on our way to work or to the pub or to the theatre are only the visible tip of the iceberg. And during lockdown, they've slipped even further down the visibility scale. When we're not going out and about, it's even easier not to see that other people are falling between the cracks.

Over the years, I've come to understand that homelessness goes far beyond living on the street. You can be homeless with a roof over your head, but if it's not a safe and secure and appropriate roof, then you're suffering from the same disease. For most young people who end up homeless, it's not because they made bad choices. It's because they didn't have any other choice.

My working life involves the exercise of imagination. Every day I sit down at the keyboard and think myself into other people's shoes. And so I set myself the challenge of imagining what it would be like to have no safe place to stay. I say 'challenge', because I've never stood on the cliff edge of not knowing where I was going to sleep that night. I've been lucky. I've been skint. I was a hard-up student, a poor trainee journalist, a broke baby writer, coppering up every month to pay the bills. But my life was never so precarious that I had nowhere to lay my head.

So I went for a walk round the city and tried to imagine what it would look like through the eyes of someone who had nothing and nowhere. You see the city in a very different way, especially in lockdown when the limited options become vanishingly few. Where can I sit down? Where can I go to keep warm? Where can I pee? How can I get new glasses? Where can I go when it's raining? Where can I wash? Who will talk to me? Is there anywhere I can get some shelter and food? How can I stop hurting? Will I ever see my kids again?

Are that bunch of drunks going to give me a doing? Will someone steal my stuff if I go to sleep?

A couple of hours of that and I felt exhausted and drained. And I knew I could make it stop any time I wanted to.

Those anxiety levels translate very quickly into mental health problems. Depression saps the will and the capacity to change. Street drugs take the edge off for a short while, but bring worse problems in their wake. It's even harder for young homeless people who don't have skills or a CV to fall back on. In lockdown, it's grown even grimmer, with no-questions-asked, cash-in-hand jobs dwindling to nothing. It's hard to see even the first step on the way out of that downward spiral for people caught in that trap. But we have to. We're a small nation and we can't afford to waste what they have to offer.

One in five people in Scotland are defined as living in poverty after their housing costs. They rely on food banks to put dinner on the table. They're just one pay packet or one car repair away from financial disaster.

We don't like to think of this as what life is like for a fifth of the population in modern Scotland. A fifth of our people whose life chances are constricted and constrained. A fifth of our people who are pushed to the margins. They don't feel part of anything. They are outsiders. They are homeless both in the literal and metaphorical sense.

That needs to change.

I want to talk a little bit about my own sense of home, because my experience leads me to believe that change is possible. I left Scotland when I was 17 because I knew I was an outsider. I didn't really understand why I felt that way. I thought it was because I wanted to be a writer and writers were supposed to have a sense of detachment. A splinter of ice in the heart, as Graham Greene put it. I didn't understand the real reason because I had no vocabulary for it.

In Fife in the late 60s and early 70s, you'd have been more likely to find a unicorn than an out lesbian. There were no templates for a life that didn't conform to narrow ideas of heterosexuality. No lesbian movies, no lesbian characters in the soaps, no lesbian sports stars. Luckily for me, in my last year at university, I found the feminists and through them, the lesbians. I found myself.

I went back to Scotland a couple of years later. I wanted to go home now that I felt at home with myself. And I discovered pretty quickly that being a woman on the newsdesk of a Scottish national newspaper was hard enough. Being an uncompromising lesbian was like living in a perpetual battlefield. The culture of the country I belonged to was, broadly speaking, misogynist and homophobic.

So I ran away to Manchester, which was a different country in more ways than one. I could be myself there. The only problem – and I know this might seem odd to some people – was that I felt I was living in exile. England is not my home. Different history. Different culture. Different sense of humour. Different sensibility. But from a distance, I saw Scotland changing. I saw a country that was having a debate with itself about what we wanted modern Scotland to be. What modern Scotland should be.

I came back to Scotland eight years ago. Because Scotland has changed. In so many ways, we have transformed ourselves. In terms of equality and social justice, it's unarguable that we have come a long way. We have a woman First Minister. We've seen political parties led by people who identify as gay and bisexual. BAME Scots are just as Scottish as the peely-wally ones like me. We welcome refugees into the heart of our communities. As we saw last year in Pollokshields, we even take to the streets to stand up for the asylum seekers who have become part of our communities.

But the job's a long way from finished. We're nowhere near as fabulous as we'd like to think we are. I won't be happy with modern Scotland till everybody who lives here has a home here. None of us should be.

It's easy to make the right noises, to say the right words. The trouble is, homelessness isn't sexy. It's not a vote-winner because, by definition, homeless people don't have a vote. There's no homeless pride march stretching through the city streets on a sunny summer afternoon. If we don't notice the damage being done to a fifth of our population, how will we notice when it's fixed?

We'll notice because Rock Trust will be closing its doors. Wouldn't that be an amazing thing?

We can choose to be better. We don't have to wait for our politicians to lead us to a better place. We all need to take responsibility for mending the broken bits of our society. We can start by noticing, by opening our eyes instead of looking away. It doesn't matter if it's giant steps or baby steps, we can all start to make the change. We can be ingenious. We can work out how to make housing a human right. How to use the resources we have to put decent roofs over people's heads. How to regulate and tax the short-stay letting that's hollowing out our cities.

How to let everyone come home.

And maybe long before the next 30 years are up, we won't need Rock Trust anymore.

Unpacking: Five Stories

JENNY LINDSAY

SHANNA, 19

packed up and flit fleeing fists fleeing
fight fleeing the smack-bang-crash of
a tight-fisted life, *he never stopped drinking*,
she explains, says, *I had to get out* before
it got to the worst place it could get
the officer ticks the box on the form
marking her *intentionally homeless*.

LILY, 24

it'll just be for a couple of nights
thanks so much — are you sure that
your flatmate doesn't mind?
i'll be really quiet not even
unpack my toothbrush
unpack my make-up
unpack my uniform, yes
i am working, yes, I'm trying, yes
it'll just be for a couple of nights,

> *no no, I understand, I'll find*
> *somewhere, sure, yeah, no bother,*
> *sorry to be in the way, sorry*
> *she got pissed off at my suitcase*
> *after only a couple of nights*
> *sorry.*

JACK, 18

from b&b to b&b to hostel to b&b to hostel to hostel
to friend's sofa to b&b to benefits withdrawn to benefits to
b&b to belongings in black bin-bags more often than in a drawer
to sleeping on the street to b&b to benefits withdrawn to b&b to
benefits to benefits withdrawn to b&b to b&b to b&b to b&b

DAVID, 21

single male of working age
no dependents, recent redundancy
assigned to a B&B with a 10pm curfew
and housing costs not covered since
he started working nights –
aye. But school him on his anger.
School him on trying harder
School him on keeping control
As he's forced into penury.
Don't talk to him of *cracks* –
Don't talk to him of *responsibility*.
To WHAT, he sighs at the uncovered light-bulb
To WHAT, he curls up, fitfully. Housed.

SARAH, 22

Simple things, really, she says — I'd like
to put a shampoo on the corner of the bathtub and
stay in one place 'til it runs out. Simple things, really,
a mattress that isn't lumpy with others uncertainty — I mean,
how many folk have stayed here before me, likes, and
cooking. Aye, cooking something that takes longer than ten minutes,
hell... I'd like ten minutes without...

She stubs a cigarette out, blowing smoke vehemently.
It curls in the half-light of the third floor window,
the view one that hundreds have had.

WICK'S STORY

I was just 16 years old when I started struggling to live at home with my mum and siblings. My mum was suffering from mental health issues and I was soon asked to leave the family home.

Living in my own tenancy, I tried to continue going to school and live what I thought was the normal life of a teenager, but the challenges of living alone meant I had to drop out. I didn't have a proper bed or a washing machine and I didn't receive any support or guidance to make a success of independent living. It wasn't long before my tenancy also broke down and I was suddenly homeless.

For a long time I was dependent on friends for a place to stay. I moved from sofa to sofa. I eventually managed to get some work in a kitchen and moved in with a friend permanently. But by then my experiences had begun to impact on my mental health. I became depressed and that led to increased isolation, and ultimately I couldn't hold the job down or afford the new tenancy and I became homeless again. So the cycle continued.

At 23, I found out about Rock Trust and sought some advice and support. My depression and anxiety had made me feel increasingly vulnerable and isolated over the years, and I didn't know how to move forward and change my situation for the better. Rock Trust referred me to the Health and Wellbeing Service for art therapy, where I benefited from weekly one-to-ones with the Health and Wellbeing worker.

In the sessions, the staff supported me with self-expression and self-reflection, through dialogue and through art. Some of the areas we explored together included family relationships, gender identity, past experiences, and the future! In addition to this support I moved into a Rock Trust tenancy, and was given additional help from one of the Housing Support workers to build my independent living skills. Things like looking after my new home, budgeting and seeking out new opportunities to help me progress in life.

I'm determined not to be held back by my past, and I'm steadily moving towards a fulfilling future. My confidence has grown considerably, and I've now decided to work towards a career in social care.

The Edinburgh Scale

KIRSTIN INNES

The snail splurged out, its phlegmy body splayed and obscene on the other side of the glass, streaked with brown like a glob of tobacco-laced spittle on a pavement. Wobbling on top was a shell the size of a baby's fist; underneath, one end of the splat tapered into a wicked-looking point while at the other two muscular eye stalks pointed – decisively, undoubtedly – in her direction.

She couldn't stop looking. She felt its presence in her sinuses. Level with her face, the snail refused to break the hold.

'What you doing, babe?'

He was behind her, warm and real in his boxers, in the kitchen.

'And how's my little duck? How are you? Good morning. Yes. Yes. That's right, I'm talking to you, my tiny love. Have you slept all night? Have you? Like a champ? Yeah!'

She cut across the top.

'Hon. Look at that.'

'Wow.' He walked to the back door, flicked a finger and thumb onto the glass, at the mucus pancake. The snail did not budge.

'I've never seen one that size before.'

He fumbled with the key in the lock, pushed up the handle, made as though to pull the door into the room.

'Don't!' she said, a high shriek in her throat. He gave her an amused look.

'Easy there. You startled him. Oh, look at that little face. Did she scare you? It's okay. Aw, it's okay, darling.'

He opened the door. The snail was now inside their house. It had crossed the threshold.

He recoiled.

'Oof. It's an invasion.'

Three other snails, none of them quite as big as their leader, were in various stages of advance up the lintel and the opaque bottom panel of the door.

'Close it! Close the door.'

He did.

'Lock it.'

'They can't open the door, love.'

'Lock it.'

He did.

'Look, do you need a rest? Let me take him for a while. Hello. Hello, darling. Are you coming to daddy? That's right. Hello there. That's right. Listen, babe, go back to bed. I can give you half an hour. I'll skip a shower.'

Under the still sweat-soaked covers, she lay flat, eyes open, smelling bodies. The rain kept up its drumming-drumming-drumming on the thin roof, just like it had done all night. Just like it had done for the last five days. Every time she closed her eyes she felt her body pitch and swerve, begin to spin a turbo-charged descent into the mattress. She kept her eyes open. From downstairs, the crying again, piercing her, pinning her down in panic.

It wasn't going to stop.

Drumming.

Downstairs he paced, shushed, creaked at doors.

It didn't stop. It wasn't ever going to stop.

She heard him mount the bottom step. The wailing rebounded off the stairwell, turning it into an amplifying tunnel. She wondered whether she could make it out of bed and into the bathroom with the bolt locked behind her before he reached the top.

'Sorry, my darling.' He was bellowing to make himself heard over the noise. 'He just won't settle for me. I can't get him to calm down.'

Her hands were pulling her pyjama top open without her consent. She definitely hadn't made the decision to do that. The keening faded, mutated into obsessive piggy snorting and snuffling, wetness, suction, release.

'Aw. Loves his mummy. Mummy makes it all better, doesn't she, little love?'

The thirst hit her, an arid rush.

'Get me some water.'

'Please.'

'Please.'

It was a pint glass, and she downed it in seconds, held it out to him. 'More. Please.'

He came and sat on the bed beside her.

'Listen baby, I think you should try and get out today. How long has it been? Have you left the house since I went back to work?'

'It's been raining like end times since you went back to work, in case you haven't noticed.'

'Well, I have, because I've been out in it.'

'Yeah. You have the car.'

'And you have wellies, a rain coat, a massive beast of a buggy and a rain hood. Come on, love. Just go to the shops or something, even? It'll do you both good.'

He walked over and opened the window. The air blew in fresh and sharp on her bare skin; the sound of the rain intensified. She broke the little pink suction seal with her finger. A rivulet of milk dribbled out onto her stomach.

'Could I just have a shower? Before you go. And go to the toilet?'

'Of course. Of course. Just let me get dressed and – no, actually, probably best if I take him before I get dressed, isn't it? Isn't it, little mess factory? You're not going to be sick on daddy again, are you? No. No you're not.'

As she bolted the door the crying started up again. She sat on the toilet, hands shoved over her ears.

'Shut up,' she muttered. 'Shut up.'

All the water had gone right through her. She wondered briefly that she was able to create this amount of urine when so much fluid was diverting to her mammary glands. The crying paraded outside the door, and he knocked.

'Babe? I think someone just wants mummy today. And I need to get to work, so –'

The pram was silver and black and huge, designed by engineers who made fast cars. A gift from his mother. It stuck in the door; she swore, pushed, swore again. There was a snail perched on the number plate by the wall. She reached out a finger. The shell was wet and gritty.

He was right. It did feel good to be out in the world. She began to head up the road towards the town centre, against the flow of water, the weight of rain beating out a gentle massage on her shoulders and back. On the breath-misted polythene pram cover a snare drum, rat-a-tat-a-rat-a-tat.

There were people walking up the street, rain-smirred outlines under dark cagouls. People she'd known before this. She didn't want to see them, wasn't ready for their faces, their peering in, their cooing.

The pram was so much bigger than her. It needed all her elbows to manoeuvre it round, up the lane out of the village, towards the farms. This was better. No humans, only crows on trees, impervious to the weather. The tarmac frayed, ruptured from underneath by tree roots and moss, marsh and bog. A snail shell crunched under the wheels and she tripped, bumped over an unseen stone, the whole contraption racing itself into mud. Wheels spun, the spokes filling with grass.

Then the crying again. Again again again. Louder and louder.

'Stop it!' she screamed at the pram.

It didn't stop.

She kicked the pram wheel.

It didn't stop.

She sat down beside the pram, on the bumpy ground, the damp seeping fast through her maternity jeans.

*

'I'm sorry, Mum, I've forgotten your name. Now, if you'll just strip him down. Yes, nappy too. He's a big boy, isn't he, Mum? Oh dear.

Oh dear now darling. There now. Ooh, the lungs on him! Oh my goodness. He certainly can scream, eh? Don't worry. There. There we go. Back to mummy. Oh this one does not want to be apart from you for a second, does he, Mum? There. There. That's better, isn't it? Oh what a mumma's boy. Let me plot this. Four weeks, yes, so he's on the 98th centile. Huge! A giant! Oh, you're happy now you're back with mummy, isn't he? Need to smell their mummies, eh? Have you thought about a sling or carrier? Some of them just don't like the pram. Might help you get out more. Get some walking done. Help those stitches heal. Your poor little perineum, eh. That was a nasty one I remember, Mum, wasn't it? A lot of blood you lost.'

The Health Visitor wiped her sanitised hands and threw the used-up paper in the bin.

That night: the chair by the cot, in the cold glow of her phone, the sucking and the drumming. Her thumb flicked and found its targets – a laughing woman with beautiful hair, slender arms and a smiling angel-child strapped to her torso. Add to basket. Tiny shopping trolley icon. Checkout.

*

Outside now, with camouflage-print straps crossing the body warmth at her chest, she could move faster, cover more ground. She followed the road up past the snail-stuck cars to what had been the golf course, before the rain had come and made marsh of the Sta-Prest lawns. Nobody here. The only noise was a deep, delicious sloshing, water rolling from hollow to pool in a new river that had carved itself along the roadside, forced the ground to shape itself differently in response. The drowned ditch plants, under glass, had been drained of their colour, made beige, but the trees planted to shield golfers from prying eyes were now outlined in moss greener than anything her eyes could remember. She needed to blink to look at it clearly. It edged its way round the gnarled branches, those ancient witch-arms frozen by a spell in the act of attack.

She bent down to the river and lapped like an animal.

*

'There's my little prince. There's my angel pie. Hello little chooka pooka. Hello Nana's boy. Oh yes you are Nana's boy aren't you? Oh I'm going to eat you all up. Yes I am. Yes I am.'

She forced her hands under the sofa cushions, under the weight of herself.

'Please just leave him in there. I've only just got him down.'

'But he wants to see his Nana, doesn't he? He wants to give his Nanawanawoowoo big cuddles. Oh yes he does. Oh yes.'

The noise was instantaneous. It split the air. Her hands were over her ears; she'd curled herself into a ball.

'Stop it. STOP IT!'

'Look now. All babies cry, hen. Ha ha! You just a bit grumpy, my wee prince? Oh dearie me. Oh dearie dearie me somebody's so grumpy aren't they just. Oh who's this little angel having a grumpy pumpy day.' This last bit bellowed.

She looked up from her knees, and they made eye contact. Mother and son. Her baby's tiny scarlet face, etched in hatred and fury through the sparkly loose-knit Lurex of her mother-in-law's jumper, struggling against the big soft body subsuming him, marching him back and forth across the living room floor. She felt every note of his rage, she knew it; he knew it in her. The noise did not stop, but she felt its frequency change in her brain, an understanding. A sweet thing for a son to do, she thought, to give voice to the wrath pulsing under her skin that she wasn't allowed to speak.

Afterwards she held him in the bath, gently rubbing his head with a soft cloth, trying to ease the plasticky floral scent away. I'm going to ask your mum to stop wearing perfume when she comes to visit, she practised saying, to the tiles. It's leaving traces on him. I don't want chemicals around him. He found her nipple and she shivered but scooped him closer, submerging their bodies under the faintly blood-tinted water.

*

The mothers group met in the church hall. On the floor, beige babies grappled with grimy primary-coloured plastic. Three toddlers fought over a large ride-on car, while a row of grandparents sat on hard chairs along the edge, averting their eyes. One of the lights futzed and pulsed, giving off a tinny wail. Buggies were lined up in the corner. The room was full of shouting.

There were two other women with babies in arms standing by a hot water urn, so she went to stand beside them. They smiled. She smiled. They took their turns, one-handed, spooning crunchy nuggets of coffee into mugs, pouring each other milk with silent nods and smiles. One of them bent forward to her.

'How old?'

'Five weeks.'

'Five weeks! Oh, look at that little face.'

Her impossibly large baby reached out a fat hand, too close too close. Automatically, a tensing, a flinching away, her arms crossing themselves over the harness on her chest.

'Gentle. Gentle fingers with the little baby, Callum,' the mother cooed.

'So small. You forget they were that little,' the other one murmured, not really addressing anyone.

She nodded, turned, crushed a squeaking toy underfoot on her way out of the door. The rain on his face woke him, but he didn't cry, just gently opened his eyes to her. She bent her head down to him and they touched noses.

'This will all be washed away. I think we need to get to higher ground,' she said.

He agreed.

*

Night-time phoneglow, sucking, drumming. Walking boots, waterproof trousers, a torch, a tarpaulin, a knife. Checkout. Checkout. Checkout.

*

'Now, there's a thing we have to do at six weeks and I'm sure you'll be fine, Mum, so don't you worry about it. It's called the Edinburgh Scale, and it's just to test how you're feeling. We do it with all the mums at this point after the birth. I'm going to hand it to you and you just tick these boxes as honestly as you can. Nothing to worry about, like I said.'

Question One, announced the paper, boldly: *I have been able to laugh and see the funny side of things.*

Four little boxes:
As much as I always could
Not quite so much now
Definitely not so much now
Not at all

They lined themselves up, along the page.
2. I have looked forward with enjoyment to things
3. I have blamed myself unnecessarily when things went wrong
4. I have been anxious or worried for no good reason
5. I have felt scared or panicky for no very good reason
6. Things have been getting on top of me
7. I have been so unhappy that I have had difficulty sleeping
8. I have felt sad or miserable
9. I have been so unhappy that I have been crying
10. The thought of harming myself has occurred to me

Over the top of the form, the Health Visitor watched her, head tilted to one side. Behind her, through the glass, a snail froze on the window, realising it had been spotted.

'Because you lost a lot of blood now, didn't you, Mum? And sometimes that can make mums feel a bit. You know. When it's on top of all this. But I'm sure you're fine. I'm sure you're fine.'

She smiled with all her teeth as she ticked the boxes. You're asking the wrong questions, she thought. You won't get me.

As much as I ever did
Not at all
Hardly at all
No, never
No, not at all
No, not at all
No, I have been coping as well as ever
No, not at all
No, not at all
Only occasionally
Never

*

In the visitor centre carpark two grey-faced teenage boys in hoodies coughed and giggled in a car filled with smoke. She shielded him from the sight of it. The cycle path round the foot of the mountain had been built to funnel sweaty neon commuters to the nearest train station, but it was now completely submerged, reclaimed by the water. A lone tern rippled over but everything else was mirror-clear, the newly-formed lake refracting gold from the morning sun, the bare trees glowing in it.

'Soup, please. Something to warm me up! Thought I'd just go for a wee walk now the rain's finally stopped!'

Too cheery? Too obvious? The woman behind the cafeteria counter just looked at her, grimly grooved mouth.

'They say it'll start again tomorrow.'

At her chest, a faint smudge of movement. She snapped off the hood and he blinked in the strip light. The grimace melted softly.

'My. But someone's fresh out the wrapper. Hello. Hello there.'

The jet of hot water screeched into the cardboard cup, steam buffeting the woman's face. She seemed unaffected. Impervious to it. She jabbed a finger at the sling.

'How old?'

'Seven weeks.'

'Is she good?'

'He's a baby.'

'Oh. Sorry. It's the – you've got some pink on him. On his hat. I wasn't to know.'

'Easy mistake.'

'Two pounds eighty-five.'

The cup juddered across the counter, white liquid speckled with green sloshing about.

'Have you got a lid?'

The finger thrust out at the pile by the till.

'Sorry. I didn't see.'

A noise in the woman's throat, like a bark.

'Eh. Bye bye, little one. Bye bye, baby boy.'

There were lumps of soup powder still sticking snottily to the sides of the cup. She grabbed a flimsy plastic stirrer, tried to battle them into dissolution. The stirrer clogged. She couldn't see anywhere to put it. At the counter, the woman busied herself stacking plastic cup holders and ignoring. The cup was too hot to hold; she grabbed a fistful of napkins to wrap round her hand and manouvered it to the nearest table, trying to keep it away from his feet.

From behind her, a hard cough. 'It costs more to sit in.'

There was a snail climbing the metal leg of the table. She breathed in, poured the scalding soup down on top of it and walked out.

The hillside was wet underfoot, slippy, but she bent low and found her own path. She only looked back once, caught her breath as the village below seemed to be on fire – no, it was just mist, the condensation rising off all those fussing bodies. She stroked his cheek and he grabbed for her finger, climbed up, up into his mossy green future.

where i feel belonging

ANDRÉS N. ORDORICA

at the peak of a wave
just before it comes crashing down
is where i feel belonging.

before the tide can push me out
or the tide can drag me in
before i wash upon the tired shore.

Cuirm-cnuic

AONGHAS PADRAIG CAIMBEUL

A' ghrian a' dèarrsadh fad na maidne
fhad's a ghabh sinn cuirm-cnuic anns an lag uaine
taobh na h-aibhne. Bha bascaidean againn,
's thug Seonag measan
agus Iain botail liomanaid a chaidh nan cop
nuair chrath sinn fosgailt' iad,
agus às deidh nam pìosan-feòla
chluich sinn, falach-fead airson greis,
agus rèisean tarsainn a' chnuic, agus leum na h-aibhne,
gus, aon as dèidh aon, dh'fhalbh iad uile,
am pàrantan gan gairm, no chionns
gun robh gnothach aca ri dhèanamh,
's choimhead mi orra a'ruith sìos a' chnuic
gus robh an lagan uile falamh,
am feur air a phronnadh, agus bloighean pàipear,
a' ghrian a' gluasad tuath 's mi dol sìos an cnoc
toirt sùil air ais gach dàrnacha ceum,
far an robh fuaim is gàire nan cleas
a' dol fhathast, gun sguir.

Picnic

ANGUS PETER CAMPBELL

The sun shone all morning
as we picnicked in the green hollow
by the river. We had baskets,
and Joan brought some fruit
and John had bottles of lemonade which fizzed
ever so well when we shook them before opening,
and after the mutton sandwiches
we played, hide and seek for a while,
and races across the grass and jumps over the water
until, one by one, folk drifted away,
called by their parents, or because they had
things to do, and I watched them running down the hill
until the glade was all empty again,
the grass a bit squashed and bits of paper lying around,
the sun moving steadily northwards as I too headed down the hill,
looking back every few yards to where the sound of games and laughter
continue to echo across all my days.

NIKKI'S
STORY

Throughout my teenage years I had a difficult relationship with my family and at 17 years of age I was told to pack a bag and leave the family home. I was on a YTS (Youth Training Scheme, on-the-job training scheme) at the time, and the staff contacted the Bridges One Door project on my behalf. They arranged to meet with me later that day and took me to the council housing office where I was presented as homeless. The council placed me in temporary accommodation in a B&B, which at least meant that I had a roof over my head.

Living in the B&B was an extremely difficult, stressful and frightening experience. I was 17 and had never lived away from home; suddenly I was in a room in a building on my own. I was struggling with the fact that my family didn't want me, and I was now living in a strange room, in a strange house and had no idea who the people were in the rooms next to me. I had to get used to a shared bathroom. I could hear other guests arguing at night and was unable to settle.

Breakfast was provided at the B&B but there was no access to cooking facilities and being on a YTS scheme I only received £29 a week to live on. My only real choice was eating takeaway sandwiches every day which were expensive, and I was always hungry. Although they put a roof over someone's head, temporary B&Bs are not a good environment for anyone to be living in long-term. I was in the B&B for eight weeks in total and although it was such a minuscule part of my life, those eight weeks were the hardest to live through.

While I was in the B&B I continued to work with the staff from Bridges One Door project to look at the different types of housing available. A Community Care Assessment was carried out and I was told about Rock Trust and their supported group-living flats. The Bridges One Door project supported me to apply to Rock Trust and I was interviewed for a place in one of their group houses. Thankfully, I was soon offered a place in a new group house that Rock Trust were opening. Were it not for YTS referring me, Bridge One Door supporting me or Rock Trust making a group flat provision, I would have ended up sleeping on the streets.

The Rock Trust group flat gave me the security and stability that I needed. I was in a group house with two other young people and a supportive flat mate who worked with the charity. The flat was different to the B&B. Us young people all had our own lockable bedrooms and front door keys. We shared a bathroom, living room and sitting room. The supportive flat mate had their own living room, bedroom and bathroom and shared a kitchen with us. We all moved into that house within days of each other, and although it was strange that we didn't know each other it was also good to have company and people my own age around me.

Unlike the B&B where I was stuck in one room, I had a place to socialise and chill out with other people. I also had access to a kitchen and my own safe space in my room. I spent 15 months living in the Rock Trust group house and during that time I was supported to learn independent living skills to prepare me for eventually moving into my own rental. At such a young age I had no experience of budgeting or paying bills and didn't know how to cook for myself or others.

Every week the housemates would meet with a support worker from the office, and we could pop into the office whenever we needed to. The supportive flat mates were there to chat to us, help us settle into a group living environment and to support us to live independently.

All of us ate together and then we would have a meeting to discuss any issues or problems in the house and what, if anything, was happening during the week. We would have a house meal once a week where a support worker would join us for dinner. The three of us young people in the house would take a turn each week to prepare the meal for everyone. We would go up to the office and be given the money for the house meal which was dependent on how many people were attending. Our budget was £2 per person for the house meal – after we had the money, we would have to do the shopping, cook the meal and have it ready for 5pm for everyone arriving. Doing something like this was a daunting task and my support worker would help me to do the shopping. To begin with they would also help me cook, but eventually with that support I was able to do the shopping and cook for a group of people by myself.

Living in the house environment with different personalities meant that we didn't always get on and agree about everything. Like with any relationships in life, arguments happened. Having house meetings enabled us to talk through difficulties and challenges with support. As a house we would do an activity once a month, where it was just us young people and the supportive flat mate. We would discuss at house meetings what the activity would be and when. Those kinds of activities allowed us to get to know each other. They allowed us to be young.

Some people would say that this type of group living is not a good environment, as you are putting people with chaotic and traumatic experiences together and risk causing even more trouble. My experience of group living was one of happiness and I can look back on my time in the supported house and smile. It gave me security, stability and a family that I needed. Family is not always blood, it can be who you choose it to be, and through my experience of group living I found my family in the two other young people I lived with. Although we have lost touch at times as life happens, I am still friends with the two other young people I lived with in 1996. Yes, you heard right, 1996! They have been with me through the good times and tough times. I never knew what to expect when I moved into a Rock Trust shared house, but looking back on it, it gave me a fresh start, a family and people who believed in me even when I didn't believe in myself.

After 15 months of living in a supported house I was nominated for a tenancy with a housing association. I was 19 when I moved into my own place – I finally had an independent home. I still received outreach support from Rock Trust for the first year. At 19, having been homeless and then suddenly having your own tenancy is still a lot to cope with. While friends who lived at home could enjoy the freedom of nights out without worry, I had to make sure my bills were paid and there was food to eat before I could even think about going out. It wasn't always easy, but I learned to budget and prioritise.

I have had to do things differently from other people I know but that doesn't mean it was all bad. I had to grow up quickly and make big decisions. I wasn't always able to do things the way that I wanted. I left school at 16 and never dreamed that I would go back to education. At 25 I went to university and paid my own way through by working alongside my studies. It was a major decision for me, and it took me longer to get there and do it than other young people as I had to make sure I was in a secure financial place to be able to afford my education. In my late 20's I also started to travel the world, and I have had so many adventures out there having been to the other side of the world twice.

I struggled throughout most of my adult life to have a relationship with my family. There were times when it was ok and times when I didn't have any contact with them. In 2007 I finally decided to walk away from them for good. As hard as that was to do, I knew it was the best decision for me. At 17 I needed someone to believe in me and to give me the confidence and skills to cope with life. I may not have known it at the time, but at 17 I was given a family and a fresh start. I can be proud of everything I have ever done, because I have done it all myself. I never had someone there to bail me out and I worked hard to be where I am today. At 19 I didn't know what the future was going to hold for me, and I think even now I still cannot believe what I have done over the years. I am still with my original landlord, although now I am in a different flat. I still hold my original tenancy. If I had been given a tenancy at 17 years of age, I wouldn't have coped with it but living in the supported group house allowed me to learn the skills I needed to succeed on my own.

When I look back today on what I experienced and what happens now I find it heartbreaking that councils are still using B&B's to house individuals and families who present as homeless. We all want and should have the right to have a safe, secure and warm place to call home. Somewhere a person can thrive. It is talked about more and there are more third sector charities supporting people, but it shouldn't be happening this way. Like anything in life, people are judged by others. I didn't choose to be homeless at 17, but that was the circumstance I found myself in. It wasn't an easy time but with care and support I made a life for myself. All I needed was a chance and I was one of the lucky few that got one.

Home

BETH GODFREY

Both static cold and dry heat foster shallow breath and cracked skin. My spine hunches and stiff hips sink into the this-will-do-for-now couch as eyes glaze over my small screen, home of too many voices. The walls enclose, confine, and even though this house is mine, it doesn't feel like home.

There is something fraudulent. Like I'm doing what I'm meant to – find bricks to stamp MINE onto. Gather trinkets and put them on display, congratulate self for how much I did or didn't pay. Pat self on back for all that's been acquired (through overwork and a constant state of being wired), and what I've had the discipline to throw away. And how all of this has supposedly made me safe.

I feel like a frog in the pot: sense the trap, its comfort.

How could this be home? Homes are living, are shared, and no multitude of house plants can muster living presence, can force 1930s stone to speak. I'm surrounded by carefully curated colours and possessions, favourite titles from formative times, and the first art I dared buy that no longer speaks to me. Even with every window and door flung wide the gap where I wish a family would be can feel like a seismic hole I skirt around carefully. My ideas of home so firmly wrapped up in other people and their laughter. Reading quietly in the same room, cooking for another's hunger, small bodies clambering into bed. Tales of clutter, sleepless nights, inevitable odours and ping ponging colds don't lessen longing. Their absence creates a void. It's a tall order to fill it for yourself. I'm scared this is it.

And the voices chime on about self-love, that by myself I am enough. That it's ungrateful to moan, sitting in my warm home.

That loneliness is a short coming, it's boring to revert to numbing. Do the reading, do the work, find out where my demons lurk. The process is its own damn prize: keep busy, be grateful, and I'll thrive.

Honestly, the best part of the day is when I leave. When I step outside and the breeze hits my cheek. My body comes alive, and I begin.

Can we really feel limitless in such enclosed spaces? Where the goal is comfort and protection from the elements. Are we not shut off? Give me shifting light, give me thunder, give me whipped hair. Buffeted by Scottish weather, I always come to rest in myself in motion, outside, senses engaged and embodied. Belonging to this land with a certainty that's been years in the making. These expanses feel like home in a way a couch and neatly framed artwork never could.

But then houses are the site of return, of dry mattresses and fast kettles, warm showers and moulded seats. How do I bring back what I've found and experienced from those sacred places? The stones and driftwood, my three antlers remind me of the rugged and intimate: Dalwhinnie, Cape Wrath, Glen Affric.

Maybe as I become more familiar with you, your body, how the old wall puckers there, where the damp gets in, then we'll grow into each other. We'll witness how the other lives that border you sometimes pierce our solitude. I wrote my dreams on the bedroom wall and then painted them over. Now they are tied up with you, and what might happen in these rooms. Maybe I'll learn to love you as I get to know you, in this commitment we've made. You are not wild and exhilarating, but you are on the edge of things, and I like that. I can walk naked in your cavities. When I wake at my most uncomfortable and vulnerable, you don't recoil. I'll begin to love your brokenness, see you less as a trap, more as a partner, with DIY battles to be fought and won and compromised over. I'll tend to you as you age, and you'll hold me when I want to be invisible and hide. You shall be a site of memories.

Home has been a place that keeps life out. How do you let it in?

Belonging

DAMIAN ASHE

Where are you from
I mean
Where are you really from
I thought I answered, really answered
Aint this my home too
I mean
How come you asking me
Not the first time but the second time
When you forced me to really answer
And I say, displaced
Cause this place
Aint the same for me as it is for you
Displaced, cause you not seeing me as I see you
This place, where you already decide is not mine.
And
Is not only you
Who have the answer before asking
Is not only you
Who decide that this one is going to speak for all
That acceptance is going to be the last thing
Is not only you who ignoring

Turning away to answer when I call

And say

Aint this my home too

I mean

How come you not asking me

How it feel when my head was on the ground

And the world saw that knee

How come you not asking me

You taking a stand

Yes, I taking the knee

But you still want to know

Where I really from

And I say no

I mean

I'm from here, there

There too

Right here where my dreams and your dreams

Come together

Right there where I presenting myself as I am

Proud to be black

There too

Black and proud

Yet you still asking the same question

Cause you think that

My dreams are different to yours

That I am going to cower

You remembering it, cowed

And I take a stand
And take the knee
And say to you
Aint this my home too?

Snow Melts

HELEN SEDGWICK

We sit in a bright room in Maryhill. The walls are papered with pictures of groups like us. In one, there are three rows, the tallest at the back, smiling for the camera. In another, everyone is dressed in bright costumes and traditional dances are captured as smudges of colour. In the corner a kettle steams, and all along the walls the windows turn foggy. The chocolate on our digestive biscuits starts to melt in our tea. We are reading Haiku.

> *snow melts*
> *and the village floods*
> *with children*
>   *~ Issa*

Next to that one is a painting by Katsushika Hokusai called 'Snowy Morning in Koishikawa'. Four women and a man sit on a balcony and point across a vast landscape of green and white to a snow swept mountain. We pass the book between us, touching the page, reading over the poem, looking back and forth from words to picture.

> *'Ah!' I said, 'Ah!'*
> *it was all that I could say —*
> *the cherry flowers of Mt Yoshino!*
>   *~ Teishitsu*

We like the spring poems, we relate to them; the blossom and frost combined, the birds and the violets, the dawn. Our group expands with late arrivals bringing snowflakes on their scarves. We pour more tea, pass round the biscuits. There's a hopefulness to spring, we say, looking to the windows that are so misty we can't see out of them anymore.

> *on the ebb tide beach*
> *everything we pick up*
> *is alive*
>   *~ Chiyo-ni*

We talk about the sea and about the beaches we remember. We describe mountains that get lost in the clouds, and the effect of the clouds parting when we finally reach the summit. We talk about home. We talk about what it means to have a home, what it means to lose one.

> *even in Kyoto*
> *when I hear the cuckoo*
> *I long for Kyoto*
>   *~ Bashō*

In summer, the colours of the paintings change. There's an intensity that wasn't there in spring. We pass the book around again, the movement creating a circle of hands. An 18th century scroll has been reproduced, the heat of the sun turning the landscape thirsty and golden. Our different accents read out Haiku with different inflections, unexpected tones.

> *the beginning of poetry:*
> *the song of the rice-planters*
> *in the province of Oshu*
>   *~ Bashō*

We are from the Ivory Coast, Iran and Zimbabwe, from Mexico, Iraq, Scotland and Armenia. We are in Glasgow, in March, and the central heating makes the snow on our coats melt in seconds. The floor has puddles; if we walk, we tread carefully, not wanting to slip. We don't know each other all that well.

> *on the water*
> *the reflection*
> *of a wanderer*
> > *~ Santōka*

Now we must write our own Haiku. That's why we're here – to write. That's why we come here every week. But today is different. We find ourselves clinging to the book of Haiku, holding on to it, turning it over in our hands. We stroke the cover, touch the orange sunset that shimmers over the water and cautiously dip our fingertips into the waves. The woman in the foreground has her eyebrows raised in a question, as though she is looking at us.

> *the beginning of autumn:*
> *what is the fortune-teller*
> *looking so surprised at?*
> > *~ Buson*

There's the sound of chairs scraping against the wooden floor, and the flicking of pages through notebooks. We write a wanderer then stop and look up, catching one another's gaze. We write the country floods. We cross it out. The ground breaks. Pages ripped. Underneath us. We start again, all of us unsure how to mold the words into what needs to be said.

> *Late autumn –*
> *A single chair waiting*
> *For someone yet to come*
> > *~ Arima Akito*

And we hesitate, as if we have no right to write in this way. We nod at each other, trying to encourage ourselves to put words on the page. We look at the photos on the walls, at the crumbs of biscuit on the table, the second hand of the clock, a half-letter of ink on a blank page.

> *'Yes! Yes!' I cried,*
> *but someone still knocked*
> *on the snow-mantled gate*
>   *~ Kyorai*

We pick up the book. We read our way through the whole year until it is spring again. And what is the fortune-teller looking so surprised at? We turn our pages over. Silence settles in the bright room in Maryhill. The central heating makes our faces flush. We write snow melts, but it's hard to know what to say next.

Embankment Tube

STEPHEN KEELER

A late October afternoon of liver-spotted plane trees, hushed galleries and tea with friends, and heading for the Tube before the rush. Something about spotting money on the ground excites me still these 70 years on. The Portland Stone was bronzed in watered light; the day was leaving, and I bent to reach the note. Even neatly folded twice with such an accuracy it had probably been meant for the coffee jar, the rent or gas or Christmas club, I could tell that it was money. Twenty quid. New and sharp, and neatly pressed as our fathers' trousers used to be.

Twenty quid. Time was I could've bought a suit: these things are what our fathers said. A note I bent to reach and looking round could see no one who might have dropped it. And so I slipped it in my wallet as carefully as it had been folded, and because I no longer have much need for ready cash, I thought no more of it, straightening my back and walking on.

Twenty quid. The Airfix kits I would have bought. An early Beatles' single, chocolate bars, a smutty magazine. A paperback, a crushpack of cigarettes. Hell, with twenty quid I could've bought a Zippo, too. These days a sleight of hand is all that's needed for transactions in the shops and bars and coffee shops I use. Money that had tingled in the hand and sparkled in the eye and jangled to the ear and spun and filled our pockets and our purses is now an e-phenomenon at counters and at barriers and turnstiles.

It is a journey I have made a thousand times. The slope, the coffee shop, the railway arch. And there's a florist on one side and a news-stand on the other and in between, the entrance to Embankment

Tube station. And on this day, a few weeks later, crouching there without a bag or cardboard sign or boxes or a bag of sorry stuff, a girl of maybe 17 or maybe 47. The adjectives come readily: the hair – lank; the skin – blotched; the hands – ingrained with dirt. And as I passed uneasily she looked and caught my eye and smiled the way the very greatest of the artists could never quite have captured. It was the smile of my first girlfriend, the one, well, you know. It was the smile of the Russian woman I met a million years ago when neither of us had the courage. And something passed between us as I stepped into the ticket hall and fumbled for my Freedom Pass and touched the twenty quid I'd found untouched since then, unused. I turned and took the three or four steps to where she sat low and pressed the note into her coarse and freezing hand.

'Oh my god, are you sure?' The only words I ever heard her speak.

'It's not from me', I said. 'I found it so it's not from me. Take care.'

The inanity struck me then and strikes me now. It's not from me. Ha! Take care. Double ha! I turned and vanished from her sight, went quickly down the steps and took my District line to comfortable Richmond – London's leafiest borough (there are tree statistics in the Town Hall) – and then, and all the way home, yes, home, I churned with guilt, the stupidity of regret, the stupidity of it all. The bloody stupidity of it. If I had been expecting to feel good about giving 20 quid to a helpless, homeless woman on the brutal streets of London, it was an opposite emotion I experienced. I felt bad about it and I deserved to feel bad about it. I will always feel bad about it.

Mermaid

JAMES ROBERTSON

I wis jist aboot awa when sumbdy I didnae ken flopped doun aside me in the daurk, and I woke up again. Flopped disnae quite dae it – she didnae seem faur aff the grund when she stertit but she hit it wi a mighty thwack. I guessed it wis a lassie fae the wey she groaned.

'Ye awright? Did ye hurt yirsel?' I wis concerned, but no that much. It wis mair like I wis lettin her ken I wis there.

'Naw, I'm fine, ta. Is it safe here?'

'Safe enough,' I tellt her. 'Safety in nummers, eh?'

That's because there wis awready fower ae us ablow the brig. It wis dry and naebdy else hung oot there at night. Maist folk wid see it as manky and dangerous, and that made it aboot as safe a place tae kip as onywhaur. No that that made it safe.

The lassie didnae answer. She jist thrashed aboot a bit as if her legs were tied thegither or somethin, and I thought, whit's that smell? Really strang, ken. Seaweed and saut and fush. Shells and saun and driftwood. It wis like a big wave had jist washed in kerryin aw that wi it, but of coorse it hadnae.

She didnae settle. I fund ma phone and shone the torch tae see whit wis gaun on.

'Hey!' she said.

'Fuckin hell,' I said.

I pit the torch aff. I didnae want the ithers wakin up and seein it. I must no hae seen it masel. I must hae been dreamin.

The lassie had a big lang fuckin fush tail, covered in scales. That's whit I'd seen, or whit I'd dreamt. Ma new neebor in adversity wis a mermaid.

We were aboot five mile fae the sea. How the fuck had she got there? Flopped for five mile? I didnae hink so.

I wis gaunae say somethin but ye learn no tae stick yir neb in whaur it's no wantit. Ye learn tae take folk as ye find them. Jist because you hink sumbdy's a mermaid disnae make them a fuckin mermaid.

So I shut the fuck up and went tae sleep.

In the mornin she wis awa. So either she wis niver there or she wis but she wisnae a mermaid. Or she wis and she wis. Fuck this, I thought. I checked ma phone. Some folk hink if ye're on the street ye shouldnae hae a phone, ye're ower puir and ower stupit and forby that ye're stervin or ye should be so how can ye afford a phone? Fuck them anaw. The signal wisnae guid because ae the brig. There wis stuff aboot a tsunami ae Covid comin at us, and tornadoes rippin through Kentucky and the Russians reddin up tae invade Ukraine but I couldnae see onythin aboot a mermaid floppin roon the toun. The battery wis low but that wisnae how there wis nuthin aboot mermaids comin up.

And then the sun shot a couple ae rays in ablow the brig, and right nixt tae me on the concrete wis a lang swirl o fush scales like a question-mark. And the sunlight hit them and they stertit skinklin, dancin, multi-coloured like a rainbow, or like sequins on a fancy frock some posh dame had slipped aff and drapped on the flair. And I couldnae help it, I smiled.

Ye dinnae dae smiles yirsel, they happen tae ye, like yawns and sneezes and greetin. The smile wis a guid stert tae the day, whitiver else wis gaunae happen in the rest ae it. I got masel up and on the move. Jen and Kyle and the guy that's niver tellt us his name were still sleepin. I stashed ma beddin and set aff tae find some breakfast and mibbe somewhaur they'd let me charge ma phone.

An Slighe

AONGHAS PADRAIG CAIMBEUL

Cha robh cinnt sam bith
gun gabhadh an t-uan
an slighe suas cliathach na beinne
far an robh Lòn na h-Eala
falaichte cùl a' chnuic.

Oir bha taghadh eile ann,
slighe cromadh sìos roimhe
gu feur uain' a' ghlinne
bha dèarrsadh òr
ann an grian an earraich.

Ach lean mi e dìreadh
far an robh a mhàthair
laighe sìos taobh nan uisgeachan
ciùin ag èisteachd ri mèilich a' pàist'
a' ruith gu far an robh a' chiad chuimhne.

The Path

ANGUS PETER CAMPBELL

There was no certainty
that the lamb
would take the path up the mountainside
where the Pool of the Swan
lay hidden behind the hill.

For there was a choice
another path winding down in front of him
to the green pastures of the valley
shimmering gold
in the spring sun.

But I watched him climbing
to where his mother
lay down by the waters
still listening to her child's bleating
running towards his first memory.

St Andrew

ANDRÉS N. ORDORICA

The herons called to me
at the kingdom's edge
where silently I stood,
                    listening.

The white-topped waves
crashed over tidal breaks
and in stillness I prayed,
                    manifesting.

The ancient amber rock
stopped time in its stratum
where uneasily I watched,
                    contemplating.

The horizon spilling over
like a map unfolding
as I cried out:

          I'm still here

wanting to return home
to a place across the sea.

A Sad Story of Home

SARA SHERIDAN

The woman interrupted story time. The children sat around Miss Monaghan who was holding the book above her head, one long finger with a close-cropped, candy-pink nail pointing to a picture of a castle and a girl on a motorbike. The rider was a princess who was setting out to rescue a prince. Arthur liked this idea. He wondered if a princess might ride to his rescue and if so, if she might arrive before the weekend, when he had to go to swimming class. Later in the story he knew the princess rescued the prince, but Arthur had his doubts about the whole affair. The prince was not allowed time to pack properly and it had occurred to Arthur on previous readings, if he was to be rescued in advance of swimming he would be sure to bring Bear Beag with him and to pack a few things in his green backpack. Some ham sandwiches perhaps, and a tangerine.

When the brisk knock came on the door, Miss Monaghan paused and the infants fell into two categories: those so focused on the story that they ignored the intrusion and the risk-takers whose interest rippled away from Miss Monaghan like a tributary sweeping off in thin rivulets.

'Miss Monaghan?' the woman said. She had short, brown hair and wore a black trouser suit. Around her neck there was a thin, gold necklace with a letter J hanging from it. Arthur thought it looked as if she had been labelled.

'I'm sorry to disturb you. I've come for Arthur Brannigan.'

The rivulets of the class's attention pooled in Arthur's lap. Miss Monaghan put down the book and inspected the identification card the woman held up.

'Has something happened?' she asked.

The woman's dark eyes flicked towards the corridor and Miss Monaghan followed her out of the room.

'You're for it now, Arthur,' James McNeil said with a sneer. A staccato rush of laughter followed the comment, then the six-year-olds fell awkwardly into silence until the door opened again.

'Arthur, you're to go with this lady.' Miss Monaghan's voice had the same tone as when somebody grazed their knee.

Without rushing, Arthur went to his peg to collect his backpack and his jacket. The woman followed to help him but he brushed her away. The class waited. Miss Monaghan looked as if she wanted to say something but she didn't and as Arthur followed the black-clad figure through the door, she resumed the story.

'I'm Jackie,' the lady said, walking slightly ahead.

The corridor was deserted. Arthur had never before noticed how shiny the floor was. He watched his feet make vague reflections on the tiles as he tried to keep up.

'Am I in trouble?' he asked.

'No, Arthur. I'm going to take you somewhere where there are toys.'

Arthur glanced over his shoulder. There were toys in the classroom. He wondered if he ought to tell her.

Outside, Jackie strapped him into the back seat of her car and swung the door shut. Arthur opened his backpack and removed Bear Beag.

'Who's that fella?' Jackie asked as she slid into the front seat and started the engine.

'My little bear.' Arthur clutched Bear Beag's thin, grizzly-coloured fur. His stuffing was wearing out and in places the nap had rubbed so much that the bear had bald patches. He'd been Mummy's when she was little. Nothing wasted, something gained.

The car smelled of newspaper and stale, sweet popcorn. On the floor there was a scatter of crumpled papers and a tatter-edged diary that

said 2017/18 on the front. 'Mummy has a bike. I have a special seat.'
He pulled his helmet out of his backpack. On the side it had a sticker
of a dinosaur with googly eyes. 'Cars cost a fortune,' he said sagely
and strapped on his helmet.

Jackie's eyes flicked towards the mirror. 'You don't need that in
here.'

Arthur didn't it take off. 'Best being safe,' he said.

The car made a clicking sound as it hovered in the middle of the road
and then turned right. Jackie drove a few streets and swung into a
car park. After a pause, she pulled smoothly into a space with a sign
above it. Arthur tried to sound out the words but his reading wasn't
fluent enough. It took time with new words. It was easier when you
knew what to expect, but he hadn't read a car space before. Jackie
helped him out of the seat and led him inside where she signed a
book beside the door. A poster on the wall showed a woman with
bruises round her eyes. Again, he began to sound out the words above
her face but Jackie touched him lightly on the back and he followed
her, this time down a short corridor and into a room. The walls were
painted pale green and there was a box of toys and, on the other side,
a short bank of chairs. Arthur clicked off his bike helmet and put
down his bag. The room felt steeped in something dark and shadowy,
like an old cup of tea that had been left on the side.

'Would you like some juice, Arthur?'

He wondered why she kept using his name. There were only the
two of them.

'Thank you, Jackie,' he said carefully.

'You can play, if you like.' She nodded towards the box.

He peered over the edge. There was a xylophone with different
coloured keys and some red rubber balls. A plastic box contained
Lego pieces. He pulled it out and sat on the thin carpet. Jackie
gave him a cup of orange squash and then perched on the edge of a
comfortable chair opposite. Arthur wondered if the cushion might

squeeze out a scream. On television it would have.

'What are you going to build?'

'A castle,' he decided, taking out a couple of yolk-yellow pieces and fitting them together. 'George likes castles.'

'Who's George?'

'A friend,' Arthur said vaguely. 'Mum says I'm allowed him until I get older.'

'An imaginary friend?'

He nodded. He didn't like to say the words because George might get offended. Instead he reached into the box and pulled out more yellow, long blocks and a few blue, square ones. 'Windows,' he said sagely.

He was fixing everything in place when the door opened and a man came in. He wore thick spectacles and carried a buff file, which was thin but from the man's posture Arthur surmised it must be terribly heavy.

'Arthur?' he checked.

Arthur put down the Lego and nodded solemnly.

'I'm Joe.' He held out his hand. As Arthur shook it, Joe took off his glasses and balanced them on his head. He sighed and sat down next to Jackie as if he was exhausted.

'I'm afraid, Arthur, there's been an accident.'

'Oh.' The word popped out of Arthur's mouth like a button off a pair of dungarees.

'Your mum was on her way to work.'

Arthur got to his feet. 'Well, we'd better go to the hospital,' he said, reaching for his backpack. Once, he'd eaten a yellow flower he'd found by the canal and Mum had taken him to accident and emergency. He'd had to have his stomach pumped. He'd been younger then and not so worldly wise. Micky Hall's brother had swallowed a whole snail last summer but it wasn't as dangerous as the yellow flower.

Joe shifted his position on the chair and the material of his trousers made a strange rustling sound as if they were made out of paper. Jackie licked her lips.

'Mum was hurt very badly. That's why they sent me to get you. We're making arrangements to make sure you're cared for,' she said.

'But she'll be worried.'

The adults looked at each other fleetingly. Joe opened the folder.

'We're trying to get hold of your grandparents,' he said. 'But it seems they don't have a telephone.'

Arthur stood up. 'Mum and I will be fine,' he said. 'We don't need them.'

Joe continued. 'In the meantime, we'll collect some of your things from home, shall we? The police have provided keys from your mother's effects. Jackie will fetch your clothes, and anything else you'd like? A soft toy, perhaps.'

Arthur pulled Bear Beag from his backpack and clutched him around the neck. Then, on impulse, he grasped Jackie's fingers with his free hand.

'You'll never find it all yourself,' he said. 'I better show you.' Jackie looked at Joe, who waited a moment, then nodded. He handed her the file and a sealed envelope.

Back in the car, Arthur stared out of the window. On the bike you had a sense of each street being different but from here everything looked the same. It was easy to ignore the traffic and the tarmac and the weather and everything when you were inside and that just left you thinking. Mum always said the bike was better than a rotten old car. Dirty old gas guzzler, Arthur thought, the words an echo of her voice that took him by surprise, just as a spit of rain landed on the glass. As the car glided along, the familiar streets looked different, as if he couldn't touch the church on the corner or the chip shop or the lines of low, brick houses packed against each other. Jackie turned the car into the colonies. It was rubbish day and the pavements were piled with dark plastic bags. Someone had put out an old hoover with its cord wrapped untidily round and round the handle, bandaged up like a mummy. Above, a savage looking seagull hovered over the slate roofs. Jackie switched off the engine and ripped open the envelope with the keys. They jingled as they fell onto the seat beside her. Mum's little torch was on the end. Arthur felt sick like the time James McNeil sat on his chest. He tried to ignore it.

'Come on,' Jackie said cheerily.

Inside, the smell of toast lingered. There was a pot of honey on the table. Millionaires don't have anything nicer to start the day. That's what Mum always said. The light on the slow cooker blinked – she had set dinner going before they left. Jackie switched it off at the socket and pulled out the plug. Mum will be furious, he thought, but he didn't say anything.

'Which are your favourites?' Jackie asked. 'Books, I mean? We should take those, shouldn't we?'

'You can leave me here, if you like,' Arthur said.

He could climb up and plug the stovies back in. In the morning Mrs Thomas from number 12 might take him to nursery. She'd done it once before when Mum was sick. 'It's like 1965,' she had reminisced, 'before the knackers moved in and everything went to hell. In those days everyone did their doorsteps properly and you knew who your neighbours were.'

Jackie crouched down. She held out her hand and Arthur took it. 'I can't leave you, silly,' she said. 'We need to get you to your granny. She'll look after you.'

Arthur decided not to tell Jackie what Mum had said about granny.

'I'd rather go to Mrs Thomas from number 12,' he said. 'Like in the olden days.'

'Mrs Thomas? Is she a relation?'

Arthur shook his head.

'Well then.'

Jackie picked up his books and went through to the bedroom. The bed gave off the sleepy odour of talcum powder and soft, creased sheets. She opened the top drawer of the chest wedged beside it. There wasn't much space, Arthur thought, especially if you weren't used to the house. It was only two rooms. Mum had rigged up a winch for her bike to stop it getting nicked from outside, and the ceiling seemed higher than usual because she was out now. Hurt somewhere.

'Did she fall off?' he asked.

Jackie closed the drawer. 'It was a traffic accident. A man drove into her.'

'Bet he feels daft,' Arthur said with a grin.

'She isn't coming home, Arthur,' Jackie replied quietly, trying to make him understand.

Arthur's fingers felt weak and a chill tickled his neck, nothing to do with the weather or the central heating or anything at all. Beyond this feeling loomed something huge and dangerous and dreadful.

'You do see, don't you?' Jackie asked.

Arthur didn't want to discuss it so he nodded.

'Do you have any questions?'

He shook his head.

Jackie opened the next drawer. 'That's mine,' he said eagerly. 'All my stuff's in there.' She took out the small pile of clothes and looked around for a bag, spotting a plastic one crushed into a jagged ball in the corner of the windowsill.

'I don't need that.' Arthur pointed at his swimming costume, which was dangling from the edge.

Jackie put it back in the drawer. 'Anyone you want to bring other than Bear Beag?'

'My toothbrush is in there.' He nodded towards the tiny shower room.

'Good boy.'

At the front door she lingered a moment. Arthur squirmed. They teased him about living in the colonies at school. Some of the kids came from the posh houses on the other side of the canal with proper hallways and big gardens. Once, Steve Lindley had come to play and they'd kicked a ball in the street with the front door open and Mum had chased off the bad boys and Steve said his Mum wouldn't let him come back because he'd told her.

'It's what we've got,' Arthur said defiantly.

Jackie nodded. 'It's a home, Arthur. That's more than lots of people manage.'

Back at the office, a policeman was sitting on one of the seats. Joe sipped a mug of tea, standing by the window. Jackie put her hand on Arthur's shoulder and raised the file as if it was a shield. The policeman smiled at Arthur who kept one eye on the box of Lego. The foundations of his castle had been tidied away. 'Go on, Arthur,' Jackie gave him a nudge, and Arthur put down his backpack and pulled off his coat. This time he chose to start with red.

'I've found a place for him at Theobold's,' Joe said.

'What about the grandparents?'

Joe shook his head. 'Constable Crilly sent a colleague.'

The policeman moved his hands slightly as if to say, there was nothing more he could do. His hands were huge like spades. Constable Big Hands.

'Can't we find a foster place?' Jackie pushed.

'You know what it's like over the summer. There's nobody taking in between here and Newcastle.'

'It doesn't matter where it is. It's going to be better than Theobold's, Joe.' Her voice was whiny. Arthur decided on a gabled roof. There wasn't quite enough Lego but he'd finish it as far as he could. Some of the roof could be in blue, which would lend a conservatory effect.

'It's only round the corner. You can visit him to keep an eye,' Joe said.

'I can drop him now.' Constable Crilly got to his feet.

'I'll do it,' Jackie insisted. 'I'll stay to get him settled. We're getting on all right, aren't we, Arthur?'

Arthur nodded without looking up.

'Get him some lunch first.' Joe looked at his watch. 'I've got to deal with the Drummond boys. They're off the rails again.'

The grown-ups looked at each other as if they had made an oath signed in blood.

'Those kids were born off the rails,' Constable Crilly said.

Arthur pushed the castle to one side but nobody commented on it.

Further into the office there was a canteen. The sound of plates clattering and the smell of long-boiled soup in the hallway laid a trail to it. Jackie chose a table and put the file and the plastic bag on a seat.

'What would you like?'

Arthur didn't feel hungry. It wasn't like him.

'I dunno,' he said.

'There's macaroni cheese. How about that?'

'And peas,' Arthur said. 'Cheesy peas,' he gave a little grin. At school there were points for eating vegetables, though it wasn't enough just to let the lunch lady put them on your plate, you had to actually eat them. The rate was one point a portion. Ten points made a coloured star and five coloured stars made a gold star. Arthur was an avid collector of gold stars. It was amazing how many you could get just by eating vegetables.

'Sit up then,' Jackie said.

She went over to the canteen, collected a tray of food and returned to lay the plate of macaroni cheese in front of him. 'There weren't any peas,' she said, 'but I got carrots. That doesn't rhyme but it might taste OK.'

There was also another tumbler of squash and a yoghurt. Jackie sipped a coffee.

'Do you want some?' Arthur pushed his plate slightly towards her.

'It's OK.' She picked up the file and started reading. This was, Arthur knew, very bad manners except on Sunday mornings. He studied Jackie's face, which he decided was like a cartoon. Earlier, she had looked alarmed and her eyebrows had gone all spiky. Now she was deep in thought, her eyes followed the line of words on the page and she kept biting her lip. You couldn't always tell what people were thinking, but Jackie's face gave you clues now and then. She pushed a short strand of hair behind her ear and Arthur imagined what it would be like if it was made of chocolate because it was exactly the right colour, and he wondered if it would melt on a hot day and if it did, whether people might rush up to Jackie and lick her melty, chocolate head. Unaware of this, Jackie checked her watch, then read a little more of the file before snatching a glance at Arthur who made sure she could see he was chewing. The macaroni was nice and it turned out he was hungry after all.

'Don't be scared,' she said. 'I'm going to try to fix this.'

Outside, the rain was on and puddles had formed all over the car park. They avoided them as they walked towards the car. Arthur climbed into his seat and Jackie strapped him in. She opened the window just a sliver and the mist on the glass began to turn into droplets. Arthur swung the palm of his hand across the pane, but it still wasn't as real as being out in the air. He kept his eyes on the slice of roof and sky he could see through the gap as the car got moving. Jackie turned a couple of corners. Arthur didn't really want to see where they were going, so he kept his eyes on the sky. At length they hit a long road with fewer roofs and gutters and more green leaves. The sky looked brighter and the rain stopped. Further still and the sun came out and trees began to throw stripes on the road. Jackie fumbled in the plastic bag on the seat beside her and pulled out one of his books. It was from the library. 'Thursday night, and this is the best kind of late-night shopping,' Mum always said when she handed over the books he'd picked for the week. Then the librarian laughed and said 'Hello, Arthur. This is a good choice. You're going to love it.' Jackie passed the book into the back. 'It's going to take an hour or so,' she said. 'Want to read?'

Arthur opened the cover but he kept his eyes on the window. The houses were getting fewer and further between. In a field there were cows and after a few minutes more, two horses grazing. Everything was green, all different kinds of green, more than you'd get if you mixed all the green crayons together. His mouth opened. Jackie watched him in the mirror.

'Never been out of town before?' she asked.

Arthur shook his head. 'I've been to the canal,' he managed, suddenly eager to chat. 'I ate a flower.'

Jackie did not seem perturbed by this information. 'Well, that's not what you're supposed to do with them.'

'I know,' he said. 'I was very little.'

After a while she turned off the road onto a smaller one. The fields weren't all green any more. Between, there were long stretches of vivid yellow that made the blue sky sing. They passed through a village with a statue beside the road that had flowers piled at its feet – dead bunches in cellophane shrouds that were overgrown with grasses and bluebells, interspersed with tatty yellow ribbon.

'What's that?' Arthur pointed.

'The Virgin Mary,' Jackie said. 'It means there was an accident here.'

Arthur strained to keep his eyes on the figure as the car drove away. Maybe Mummy would get an accident statue, he thought. It was odd there weren't more statues because people had accidents all the time. Last week Miss Monaghan had broken the DVD player.

Jackie fiddled with the radio knob but nothing came out except crackling. She sighed. After a while she pulled in and looked at the buff file again and then the car's indicator clicked as she got back on the road. Further along she swung left onto a lane that was like a tunnel. Grass and hedges grew on both sides and it made Arthur think of the neon green pinball machine at the swimming pool that he was never allowed to play even though it looked a lot more fun than getting water up your nose.

Now and then the hedgerows split at the entrance to a field. It was as if the world was playing hide and seek. The car slowed behind a tractor that turned off into a farmyard. Jackie waved at the driver before she continued round some bad bends and downhill where he caught sight of a slash of sea in the distance as if some impossibly blue paint had spilled over the view.

Then at last, the car slowed as Jackie turned into another farmyard. It was a nicer place than the tractor had gone into, Arthur thought, with a row of stables and a field with a flash of nut-brown chickens running back and forwards. A pale, ginger cat lazed in the sun in front of the gate, its tail flicking back and forward like the second hand on a broken clock. It pointedly ignored the little dog that ran up to the car and barked in greeting.

'You stay here, Arthur,' Jackie said, and she petted the dog as she got out of the car.

Arthur wasn't sure what else she expected of him. He fumbled at the strap that held him in place but it wasn't easy to undo. The dog seemed torn between following Jackie to the front door of the stone farmhouse and remaining next to the car. Bored, the cat looked away as the dog made his decision and bounced towards Jackie's heels. When the front door opened, Arthur could just about make out the old man's face. Jackie showed him her identification. The dog began barking again and Arthur thought it was because the man was barking too, or at least, that's what it looked like. Then the door slammed shut. Jackie didn't turn round. Arthur saw her take a deep breath and ring the bell again. When nobody came she glanced back at him and disappeared around the side of the farmhouse with the dog so keen to follow that he almost tripped her up.

Arthur wound down the window. There was an animal smell on the air that he didn't recognise – hay from the horse stalls and manure. It smelled both wet and dry at the same time. 'Hello pussy,' he called to the cat, whose tail paused momentarily mid-quiver.

He heard the big girl before he saw her – the sound of whistling that seemed off tune and the scrape of a gate on the other side of the stables. She stopped, holding a black bucket in her hand that continued to sway. She was wearing wellington boots and a long, purple jacket. Her hair was auburn, plaited down her back and she had blue eyes and only one or two freckles, but big ones.

'Hello,' said Arthur. 'I'm Arthur.'

'Rachel,' the girl announced. 'Are you looking for somebody?'

Arthur wasn't sure. 'They've gone into the house,' he said.

Rachel pulled a roll of pastilles from her pocket. 'I like the lime ones,' she admitted cheerfully as she removed a green sweet that was on top and offered him the orange one next in line.

'Thanks.' Arthur put it in his mouth.

'I've got to feed the chickens. Want to come?'

She unbuckled him and helped him out of the car. The bucket was half-full of brown pellets. 'Here,' she said, putting it on the ground in front of the gate, 'take a handful.'

The pellets felt satisfying between his fingers.

'Got some?'

He nodded.

'Right. Throw it over.'

As the chickens came rushing towards him, he panicked, flinging the feed and turning away immediately. The girl laughed. 'It's OK. They can't get through the wires. Here,' she held out her arms. Arthur let her pick him up. She offered him the bucket again and this time, throwing the feed over the fence didn't feel so scary. The chickens fluttered and pecked and shoved each other and one of them let out an indignant cluck as it tumbled over. The girl offered Arthur the bucket again and this time he angled the feed to make the birds spread out. Rachel was warm and she smelled like milk. He felt bruised, he realised, like the day he and Mum had bought peaches and the flesh was too soft. Like the lady in the picture at Jackie's office. Suddenly he wanted to disappear under the girl's purple jacket, as if he was Bear Beag in an inside pocket.

'What's that, over there?' Arthur asked, pointing at some little huts on the other side of the field.

'Those are the bees. We make our own honey. Millionaires don't have anything nicer to start the day.'

Arthur grinned. He felt as if he could disappear inside this girl – melt into her so completely that they'd become one person, but she put him down and poured the rest of the feed over the gate. 'If you like,' she said, 'I'll take you to see the horses. If your mummy doesn't mind.' She glanced at the house.

'My mum's not here.'

'Your daddy then?'

Arthur didn't like to explain. The girl took his hand. 'Let's ask. Are they inside?'

The front door wasn't locked. The two of them stopped dead as they stepped onto the carpet. Rachel looked at Arthur and he returned her stare. There was shouting coming from further inside, behind a closed door.

'That little tike's not our responsibility!' It was a woman's voice and she sounded furious. 'He's illegitimate! What would everybody say?'

'He's your grandson, Mrs Brannigan.'

'We told Bella at the time she couldn't live here – not unless she gave him up – and she made her decision. We don't know the child and we don't want to know him, isn't that right, Dickie?'

Dickie didn't answer. It was Jackie's voice that cut in next.

'You've lost a daughter. Please consider carefully before you lose a grandson. Once a child is in the system, it's difficult to get them out. That's the reality. What do your other children think? You have other children, don't you?'

The woman sounded proud. There was an edge to her tone, a fierceness. 'I have four children. Two of them married in London; one still at home. She'll be gone soon and she doesn't need *this*. She has *exams*.'

'Jesus, woman,' a man's voice took over. Dickie at last. 'I can't hear myself think. Be quiet, would you?'

Rachel sank onto the bottom stair and pulled Arthur with her.

'Is your mummy Bella?' she whispered.

Arthur nodded. The big girl's eyes filled with tears. 'Oh God,' she began to sob. 'You're my nephew, wee man.' She ruffled his hair. 'The disgrace without a proper dad.'

'Dads are over-rated,' Arthur said with a wink. It was what he always said when people pushed him to talk about it. Mum had said it once.

'I saw you before they chucked her out. You were a tiny baby and I was ten or something,' Rachel continued. 'I suppose she must have been the age I am now.'

In the back room there was a scraping sound – a chair pulled across tiles. 'We told the police this morning.' The woman's voice was insistent. 'We said no.'

Jackie's tone remained calm. 'I know I shouldn't have come, but he's a lovely kid. This has turned his life upside down and he doesn't even know it yet. If you'd just say hello . . .'

Rachel's eyes narrowed. She stood up, walked across the hallway and opened the door. Arthur wasn't sure what to do so he stayed put. He laid his palm on the carpet, feeling its roughness, letting the fibers prickle his skin. Over the threshold there was a worn kitchen table. Jackie was standing on the other side of it with the old man who had answered the door almost beside her and an old, grey-haired lady sitting down. On one wall there were pictures of horses. Rosettes in bright colours were stuck to the front of a large fridge.

'This is ridiculous!' the girl snapped. 'He's Bella's kid. What the hell is wrong with you?'

'That's enough of your cheek, young lady,' the older woman growled but Rachel wasn't to be put off.

'All you care about is what people think. That's more important to you than any of us. You chucked Bella out just when she needed you and now you're going to do the same to her kid. No wonder we all wanted to leave. No bloody wonder.'

The man looked as if he might explode. His neck turned bright red and he gave a low grunt. 'Maybe we did the wrong thing, Eleanor,' he said. 'I'm not so sure any more.'

'You could just meet him,' Jackie cut in. 'You'd like him. He's a good kid.'

At the table, the woman let out a dismissive puff of air and Arthur was surprised when this was superseded by a sound coming from somewhere deep inside him. It felt like a solid block made out of stormy weather, welling through his stomach and into his chest and then opening his jaw and stretching his lips and turning into a wail. The dog that had followed Jackie into the house dropped onto its haunches under the kitchen table and Jackie rushed forward.

'Oh, Arthur, I'm sorry, pet. I thought you were in the car.'

She was no comfort. Arthur couldn't see the kitchen any more. His scream had obliterated it. He heaved a breath and suddenly his eyes focused on a small oak table in the hallway with an untidy pile of ragged-edged letters on top. The wail continued for a moment and then changed key into a sob. Arthur gasped, greedy for air. He pointed a finger but it seemed like someone else's finger. Ahead, on the wall, there was a picture of his mum with some other kids. She looked different, but it was her in a school uniform with a dog jumping for a treat she was holding up high. She was smiling, her head tilted back, her hair longer than it really was. It looked as if she had dressed up. 'There she is,' he managed to say. And then words were no longer possible and he went back to bawling because he'd realised now. He knew. The grown-ups in the kitchen just stared.

Then the man walked right past Jackie as if she didn't exist and grasped Arthur by the shoulders. His fingers were long. They had a scattering of white hair like the patches of snow that had fallen on the pavement last winter.

'It's all right,' the man said. 'What's his name?' he asked over his shoulder.

'Arthur,' Jackie said. 'He's Arthur.'

'Well, then, Arthur. I'm your grandad and you'll be all right now. You're home. This is where your Mummy comes from.'

Arthur's chest juddered. 'But they said she's not coming home,' he managed to get out.

'I know, son.' The old man followed Arthur's eyes to the picture. He took it off the wall and placed it in Arthur's hands. 'That was her final year at school with her brothers and sisters. Right before she had you. She was brought up here, you see. That's the front door right there, in the background.'

'Dickie,' the women in the kitchen chided her husband. 'We don't even know who the father is.'

The old man cast a cold kind of glance over his shoulder. 'For God's sake. He's Bella's boy. Look at him,' he cut her off. 'He's here now, that's the thing and Rachel's right – what does the father matter?'

'I'll help,' Rachel said, 'I promise I will.'

'Like you were going to help with the new pony?' The old man's eyes softened as if he'd made a joke. 'You'll leave Arthur to me, isn't that right, Arthur?'

Behind him, the woman's lips stiffened and she made a guttural noise. She peered at Arthur and sat down but the old man had made it up his mind.

'I won't hear it, Eleanor. Do you understand me?'

The woman looked away. She bowed her head, only a fraction.

Everybody relaxed as if a little bit of air had been let out of a balloon that was about to burst. Rachel smiled and crossed her arms.

'Thank you, Mr Brannigan,' Jackie said. 'We found Arthur a care place but his best chance is here. That's the truth of it.'

'Of course it is. My wife was hasty this morning. It was the grief.'

'I'll get his things from the car.' Jackie disappeared through the front door. When she came back she put the bag and the backpack on the carpet and handed Arthur Bear Beag.

'Thanks,' he said.

'I'll write up the paperwork.' She put out her hand to shake Mr Brannigan's. 'They'll assign somebody from the department down here to keep an eye on things. They'll help you sort out the school. Goodbye, Arthur,' she said, crouching down. 'Be a good boy.'

Through the open door, Arthur watched her leave. As the car pulled off, the ginger cat stalked over to the stable where he sat licking his paw. The lady put a cup into the sink. Her mouth twitched and her eyes narrowed, as if she'd tasted something and she couldn't quite decide whether she liked it or not.

'I suppose he can stay in Bella's old room,' she said. 'But don't expect me to like it.'

Grandad Brannigan touched his wife lightly on the shoulder. 'Things change, Eleanor,' he said.

'Can I take Arthur to see the horses?' Rachel asked.

'If he wants to go.'

Arthur put down the picture of his mum and tucked Bear Beag under his arm.

'That was your Mummy's bear.' The old man smiled so that his skin crinkled.

'On Saturday there's this swimming class,' Arthur started. It had been on his mind. He shouldn't have left his swimsuit behind. That had been naughty.

Grandad Brannigan sounded apologetic. 'Sorry, son, we won't run to swimming classes. Next summer I'll teach you at the beach if you like. The water's cold but it's where your mother learned.'

Arthur got to his feet and took Rachel's hand. He was glad his scream had disappeared. He hoped it didn't come back. 'I didn't really like swimming,' he admitted. 'It was too complicated. But I'd like to see these horses. Maybe one day, now I'm staying here, I'll learn to ride.'

A Sair Time Comin

JAMES ROBERTSON

Oh whaur hae ye been, ma dearest ane?
Oh whaur hae ye been, and are ye come hame?
I hae stauchered and strayed up vennels and closes,
I hae stood on the ledge and looked doun at the watter,
I wis oot in the cauld but I burned wi a fever,
I wis pit in the cells for consortin wi strangers,
I hae slept wi the deid in a thoosan auld kirkyairds,
And it's a sair, and it's a sair, oh it's a sair, aye it's a sair,
It's a sair time that's comin.

Oh whit did ye see, ma dearest ane?
Oh whit did ye see, and are ye come hame?
I saw hunkerin men like sodgers in trenches,
I saw weemin wi misery etched on their faces,
I saw folk gettin bevvied and folk that were stervin,
I saw beggars wi dugs and naebody carin,
I saw streets fou o shops that shone like cathedrals,
Their windaes were mirrors but the gless wis aw broken,
And it's a sair, and it's a sair, oh it's a sair, aye it's a sair,
It's a sair time that's comin.

Oh whit did ye hear, ma dearest ane?
Oh whit did ye hear, and are ye come hame?
I heard a burd sing in the hert o the city,
I heard chainsaws roar in the mids o the forest,
I heard orchestras playin and missiles explodin,
I heard diplomats screamin and scientists prayin,
I heard an auld spaewife, 'I tellt ye, I tellt ye,'
I heard an auld bodach, he couldna stop greitin,
I heard a young lass, she wis rantin and ragin,
And it's a sair, and it's a sair, oh it's a sair, aye it's a sair,
It's a sair time that's comin.

And wha did ye meet, ma dearest ane?
Aye, wha did ye meet afore ye cam hame?
I met some that were ghaists and some that were hauntit,
I met bairns that had drouned in the deeps o the ocean,
I met teachers wi guns and dreamers wi banners,
I met peacemakers wadin in bluid tae their oxters,
I met a dictator, he said he wis sorry,
I met a protestor, she said she wis Jesus,
And it's a sair, and it's a sair, oh it's a sair, aye it's a sair,
It's a sair time that's comin.

Oh whit'll ye dae noo, ma dearest ane?
Aye, whit wull ye dae, and wull ye bide hame?
I'll awa tae the dreich and desolate places
Tae yowl at the mune and brek breid wi a stranger,

I'll stravaig in the widds and hoot wi a hoolet,

I'll drink fae the pool o the saumon o wisdom,

I'll seek oot the licht in the bield o the mountain,

I'll gang tae the shore and collogue wi a selkie,

I'll staun at the lip o the loch wi a heron,

Syne I'll look tae the lift and the greylags abune me,

Cryin their news ower the touns and the clachans

Whaur hauden-doun people are waukin and roosin,

The hameless, the hermless, the seik and the stricken,

But gin they're tae thole or gin they're tae rise

It's a sair, and it's a sair, oh it's a sair, aye it's a sair,

It's a sair time that's comin.

Hurt

ANDRÉS N. ORDORICA

1. the air felt cool
like sweet nectar

2. felt sturdy yet ethereal
(see: delicate; breakable)

3. At the centre of pitch
darkness: black plum

What I need the most
is to float on air

The light is opposite—
hurting destroys my delicate body.

Hurt is not a home.

TARA'S STORY

Every one of us has had to deal with challenging situations throughout our lives; some maybe more than others, but it's how we deal with and overcome these hurdles that's paramount. For many of us that is a lot easier said than done – I have certainly found it easier to say than to do. Here I want to share with you something that is very personal to me, my journey over the past seven or eight years, and how I was able to navigate the darkest times.

I want to start off by giving you an insight into who I am, so here goes: I am a 22-year-old female that suffers from severe mental health problems. I live with these problems as a consequence of the challenges I have faced. I've been homeless; I've been both physically and sexually abused. I felt so low as a consequence of this that I couldn't see an end in sight, no light at the end of the tunnel. As far as I was concerned, the only ending I could see at that time was one that I made happen. It brings a tear to my eye to write that but it's the truth. I felt so low and alone and had such strong suicidal thoughts that I was scared of myself, but now, looking back, it was the final push that I needed to realise that I had to get help before it was too late. Thankfully for me, Rock Trust became involved in my life at the right time. I can honestly say with my hand on my heart that if I had left it for even another few weeks then I would not be here today to share my story with you.

It was back around the year of 2016 when I met with Rock Trust for the first time. I was homeless and living in a youth hostel which was daunting enough, but to then find myself in a situation where I wasn't getting any money and had no one to turn to for help, it was crucial I got some urgent support Everything that was going on in my life at that time was so new and raw to me that I was incredibly grateful when Rock Trust allocated me with a personal support worker. Her name was Amanda, she met with me on a weekly basis to support me in areas that were challenging and to provide me with the resources to make life that bit easier. She had such a friendly vibe about her and was so easy to talk to that I was able to build a trusting relationship with her quite quickly. Trust is something that I have always found challenging, so I was actually surprised with myself how easy it was for me to establish that with her. Amanda supported me in getting benefits in place, corresponding with other professionals such as the council, and getting me my first ever tenancy. No matter what the issue was she supported me, and we dealt with it together as a team. For the first time I didn't feel alone, and life was beginning to feel a little less daunting. But that was soon to change.

A few months into my support the absolutely unthinkable happened, causing my life to literally be turned upside down… I was sexually assaulted. I became broken. I felt worthless and didn't know what to do or how to cope. I was on my own, I didn't have family in my life to provide me with the emotional support that I desperately needed. I felt so isolated and vulnerable and I couldn't manage even the easiest of day-to-day tasks. Amanda was still there to offer help but she wasn't trained to provide me with emotional support. She became increasingly worried about my well-being and suggested that she introduce me to her colleague for extra support. I'm not going to lie, my first thoughts were that yes, I was struggling, but I wasn't a toy: I wasn't broken and I didn't need someone coming in judging me, I didn't need to be fixed! But I'm thankful now that she soon managed to convince me. Together we met with her colleague Bel, a trained therapist who also worked at Rock Trust. We discussed a range of ways that we could try to improve my mental health. They were all interesting, but I was immediately drawn to art therapy and decided I would give it a try. The idea of getting help through doing something I love appealed to me. I was always creative and from a young age I loved doing art, so this form of support seemed to be a good way to move forward, and it most definitely was.

I met with Bel one-to-one on a weekly basis and I loved it from the beginning. She had such a caring nature and I got on with her from the start. Truth is, I was still broken, so it took me a while before I was able to open up completely, but the more I engaged with her the easier it became, and before I knew it I was opening up about all the pain and heart ache in my life. It wasn't long before I started seeing the benefits of engaging in these sessions. I could walk into a session and be in the worst mood ever, but together we would make a piece of art and maybe shed the odd tear or two, and at the end of it I would feel like a different person - lighter, as though a weight had been lifted off my shoulders. Others could even see the difference that one hour made to my mental health. I was excited to go to my art therapy sessions every week and I continued to engage in them for around a year. It helped me in so many different ways. I also learned a lot of skills and coping strategies that I was able to use in different situations to prevent myself from falling into such a bad place again. Before I knew it my block of sessions was over, but I was fine with that, for I could see the difference within myself and felt ready to go it alone again. I continued to use the skills and resources that both Bel and Amanda had given me, but around four years later that all changed as I came crashing right back down again.

I had hit rock bottom, I thought that my life was hard before but this time it was different. I had tried to apply what I had learned but it didn't work. I mean I can't actually put into words what I felt or why these things didn't work: all I can tell you is I realised within myself that I had to get help. I knew that if I didn't do something soon it would have been too late, so I decided on my own that I had to do something, and after having such a positive experience before I decided to reach out to Rock Trust again. I knew it was a long shot, but I also knew that there would be no harm in trying, so with this in mind I made the decision to phone them and explain what was going on in my life and see what they could do to help. Thankfully they gave me an appointment to go and meet with a crisis worker the following week. I was so relieved and grateful for this.

I soon met with Kerry – she was one in a million – I shared with her in detail what was going on in my life and the struggles I faced on a daily basis. She went above and beyond to help me, constantly corresponding with a number of different parties and exploring a number of different resources but at times we felt we weren't getting anywhere. We agreed that I would benefit from art therapy sessions again, and she discussed my case with her colleague Emma who was happy to meet with me. Emma and I met straight away and didn't waste any time, beginning our sessions immediately. It didn't take long before I started to see the benefits of working with her, but unlike the last time this was slightly different: my mental health was so far gone that I had good days and bad days, I still do, but we took each day as it came and dealt with it together. She provided me with the emotional support that I needed while Kerry worked in the background, liaising with other professionals and supporting me through my crisis. At times we thought that it was never ending, but we did get there and I no longer get support from her. I am still engaging on a weekly basis with Emma and I love it. I do still have both my good and bad days but I also see how far I have come over the period we have worked together. Emma is such a loving and caring soul and I look forward to meeting with her every week. She is like my best friend and I trust her with everything.

I have always been scared to ask for help, but Rock Trust have taught me that it's not a crime. If anything, it shows courage and determination. I have always said that I wouldn't be the person I am today without the support Rock Trust have given me and, yes, I still stand by that 100 per cent. But they have also made me realise that it is as much down to me as it is to them, as it was me who engaged in these weekly sessions and it was me that showed the strength and determination to succeed. Emma encourages me to reflect back to the darker times but in a positive light – if I look back today on how I was when I reached out for a second time to how I am now I can acknowledge the progress I have made. Looking back, I see a broken and fragile woman without an end in sight, but now I see someone who is determined and strong and that is thanks to the outstanding team at Rock Trust. They showed me a huge amount of warmth, kindness and respect when I was at my worst, but, most importantly, they have also given me the support to help me find the confidence that I was missing. They helped me realise my full potential and believe in myself, which is something that I have not been able to do in a very long time. Hand on my heart, without them I know I wouldn't be here to share my story with others, but thankfully I am, and I hope that by doing so I might help them too.

I don't know who you are that is reading this, but I guess you are either a young person that has entered hard times or a kind-hearted individual that has donated or is considering making a donation to Rock Trust. If you are a young person that is struggling, please reach out and don't be afraid to ask for help. If you are anything like what I was then I know that this is easier said than done, but take it from someone that has been there: it really is the best thing you can do. Nobody will judge you and there is no crime in admitting your struggling. You will get there in the end. My advice to you is to be honest with yourself and with whoever is around you offering support, because that is the first step to building a better future. Always know that what works for one person may not work for you, but I can assure you that exploring all of your options will help you find what will, and then you are half way there. Rome wasn't built in a day and things do take time, but I am sure that somewhere inside you there is still a fight left to be fought, and I wish you well in your recovery.

If you are reading this and have made a donation to Rock Trust or are considering making a donation then I personally want to thank you, as without your generosity the amazing work that Rock Trust do would not be possible. I am only one in a huge amount of young people that they have been able to help, and that is thanks to you.

I am honoured to be given this opportunity to share my story with you and to help The Rock Trust celebrate the huge milestone of thirty years. What an amazing achievement. It is remarkable to think about how many people just like myself that they have managed to help.

Fridge

ROCK TRUST YOUNG PEOPLE

With the persistent tick of the clock,
mind blank
and a heaviness, limbs like lead,
I trudge begrudgingly over to the fridge
again.
A slug.

Eyes squint as the artificial white light
floods the dark kitchen.
I'm met with a hollow reception:
an orphaned piece of cheddar,
hardened over time and
cowering in the corner,
has given up;
older than the fridge itself,
a defiant bottle of Worcester Sauce,
the gatekeeper in the doorway,
is judging my every move;
and, centre stage, captivating,
glowing like a stained-glass window,

sticky and sultry

a jar of marmalade.

Disappointed but not surprised,

with a swing of the door

the kitchen returns to darkness,

the fridge and its inhabitants silenced.

I shuffle back to the warm embrace of the couch.

With a click of a button

the binging resumes:

Man Vs Food.

Pluripotent

JENNI FAGAN

She lost her virginity last Friday uhn it was shite. It wasnae shite because it hurt or cos she was too high to remember why she thought it hud been a good idea tae lay down, except the stars had looked prettier than she ever had seen. It wasnae shite because she didnae wait tae do it wi some cunt she loved, or even someone who she felt a wee bit comfortable wi, or even someone she knew for that fact. Louise doesnae give a fuck about any ay that. She's observed the so-called adult world for years and has no delusions regarding happy ever afters, movements in the Earth or any of that other pish. It was shite because he filmed it and he never said he would and after she stood up she felt like a bit of his thing had fallen off and that it was still in there.

No-one telt her that happened.

Perhaps it would come out later.

Too embarrassed to ask her sisters, who would only say – *if yer old enough tae spread yer legs then ye should ken aw they hings!* She spends the first three days in pain but like maist hings it subsides leaving residual embarrassment uhnna fuckload ay confusion.

Also, a tiny wee part ay her, a much ignored, resented part keeps oan repeating at random; you didn't even wait till you were thirteen.

Ye threw it away on a cherry-hooked-closet-junkie-prick uhn even if ye said noh, he ken't ye meant aye – cos you wear manky-hoor all fucking ower ye.

It was shite.

It's all shite.

Today she is thirteen and this morning her Ma gave her a silver

89

necklace wi a heart on the end. She kissed her at the breakfast table and looked kind ay teary and she wasnae even pished. Tonight she'll go hame after school uhn act surprised at the bought cake and her older sisters will stand around bitching in the kitchen but they'll be nicer than usual which means they'll just be averagely disinterested. She keeps touching the necklace to make sure it's still there. She finds the feel ay cold metal underneath her shirt reassuring. All the way tae school she scuffs her feet uhn it makes a gentle swooshing sound on the wet pavement. The lead feeling in her spine gets mair intense the nearer to school she gets until she feels her back must be stooping and people in the street urr staring cos she is a total fuckin freak.

The three girls in 2c that said they're going to kick her head in and film it dinnae ken she's got a wee knife in her pocket. A wee knife her ma used tae use tae cut open letters when she still was in her mail-opening years. Now the debt collectors ken them aw by name but the mail never gets opened anyway. The knife is the shape ay a fish at the top uhn she likes the feeling ay cold metal in her pocket uhn after him filming her she's no fuckin having any mair close ups ay her ain face in fucking pain. She'll no need tae use it. They'll no dae anyhin. If they do though. She turns it ower in her pocket and they are up ahead by the school gates smoking so she swerves sharp left and wriggles her way into the middle of a bush.

It is a fuckin indignified place tae spend yer day but it isnae as bad as sleeping in them and she's done that plenty ay times already. Louise doesnae feel twigs scratching her legs and hands as she pushes in. She is numb wi cold and a heavy emptiness sits inside her, growing more dense ivvry day. She struggles tae pull out a Regal that she'd stubbed oot earlier, she can smell the rich burnt metallic scent fae her pocket and oan her fingers as she lights it. It takes three matches. Each sizzles out and dies. Her fingers are numb and look like raw chipolatas fae the cold. It's fuckin baltic. Oan the third shaky strike she catches a blue flame like a fuckin moment ay magic on a dying earth. She inhales. A fleeting victory! If anyone stood far enough up the hill behind the school they'd see smoke coming oot the top ay the bush. Naebody climbs up there but, except firrit night tae get fucked or ivvry Friday eftir school fir a fight. Her legs urr covered in goose pimples. It's October but she's still wearing summer clothes because the only winter coat she owns is a skanky duffle. Her physics teacher has one like it. He's such a fuckin paedo. He took a class yesterday morning on how long it would take baith a feather uhnna car, dropped at the same time, tae hit the ground.

She wanted tae say that he should try weighing varying sizes of emptiness.

There was nae speaking though.

No fae her mouth.

Emptiness is fucking heavy but. Oppressive. It has surround-sound devastation and keeps weighing in more each day. Louise has an empty chasm in the middle ay her chest, s'probably where a heart should be, ay. It grows heavier by the day. Nuhin shifts it. Not throwing up. Not E's. Not speed. No even smoking till she whiteys uhn leaves her body behind tae panic her way aroond space. She did that on the Friday after he'd went away haim fir his tea. He works fixing motors. Everyone hinks he's cool. He'd glanced back at her wi a wee smirk. Hud what he wanted ay. Hud it and woudnae want it again. Between her legs it still felt like a bit ay him hud fallen off uhn she had never felt scared by her own anger before but for a second she wanted tae take oot the pen fae his shirt pocket and stab him through the eye, stick it in deep uhn twist it slow-as-fuck and then walk away throwing over her shoulder her ain cool non-committal smirk. She didnae. These urr fantasies that ayeways come later. She replays them at leisure adding a flourish here, an extra cool cutting biting remark there – always she comes out on top, clear, concise and hard as fuck. It's nuhin like reality. It has been three months since it happened now and he husnae spoke tae her again.

Louise watches the girls going intae class.

Resists the urge tae boak.

It's rising up in her throat though.

She takes dry crackers oot ay her bag and nibbles on yin. The lassies urr already in the Home Ec department. She can see them through the big windows like she's watching some play at the West End or suhin. The hing is if they try tae batter her as a collective. In two's she can take them. Easy. Really – aw she wants tae do is bake a nice cake in Home Ec and go haim tae watch that new K-pop band she saw online this morning.

The class is quite empty.

Louise watches it fae the bush like she's in a wildlife documentary inspecting the social world of radges. Aw the lassies that hate her arrange themselves on tables wi their shorter than short skirts. They re-apply lip gloss. Gie stabby flirty glances tae ivrry cunt that comes near them. They posture and pose sticking their flat tits oot and ridin their skirts high as they can. They roll their eyes and look practices-perfect bored. Louise pictures them naked and licking each other oot cos they aw hink they urr so fucking amazing. Nasty, entitled, self-obsessed fake cunts. Living in fear ay them isnae an option. Avoidance is only a survival strategy fir now cos her body needs her ay. It is a long double Home-Ec lesson standin in a fuckin bush.

An entire pack ay fags later – Louise shuffles backwards oot ay the bush.

Should probably quit the smokin ay.

The bell is ringing.

A long branch slaps her eyebrow as she goes back ontae the path (like she's been on it aw the time) like she's no some kind ay random weirdo skiving bush dweller. She touches her face. Blood. A tiny shock ay colour on a bleached-oot day. The sky is white and the pavement grey. Trees hold bare twigs aloft. Ower a thousand assorted schoolies pour toward the chippie uhn the garage. She keeps her head doon. Picks her way through the crowd. On the Friday when he did it she hud went and stood in the bus stop to come hame and it wiz rainin uhn she'd smoked joint after joint till she couldnae feel the E anymore – all her limbs just turned into a big angel delight sogginess that crumpled her until she lay on the floor of the bus stop staring along the road.

The road was slick and wet wi rain.

Streetlights were reflected in it like shimmering orbs.

Every time a car went by it sent a little tidal wave through the reflection distorting orange light outwards yet it always contracted back to the original round shape. Louise felt already that she too could distort her mind and body with chemicals as much as she chose but the shimmer would ayeways wear off and she too would have tae come back tae her original shape, self, reality – again and again. The leaves on the forest floor are wet and soggy so she walks until she finds a flat tree trunk to sit on. She smokes three mair fags in quick succession, double-drawing each yin for a cheap and easy morning buzz, then she scrunches up the packets and decides that's it. Nae mair ay that. They're rank as fuck anyway. During her homework tutorial hour on Tuesday she went online pretending tae find oot stuff fir class but really it was so she could look up the cellular development of a foetus. It turns out the human desire tae form itself out ay cells into a functioning mammal is so strong, that it begins in fact fae the first embryonic instant. The heart that she feels beating now against her chest may in fact not be the first heart she, as a group of cells, manufactured. It may be the second or third or perhaps even fourth heart, the others – deemed not good enough or strong enough would have been discarded as the cells tried again and again to regroup into the strongest healthiest version of themselves possible. She is the result of the most perfect amalgamation those cells could muster.

Somehow she feels cheated.

This is only because she cannot see her eyes are pretty and she may be somewhat plain compared to other people but she has an honest face and an athlete's shape. She feels ugly. No good enough. Strives always for a more perfect version of herself. She understands this drive well. She continuously betters herself in subtle ways such as stopping biting her nails and giving up eating chocolate to clear her skin and further whittle down a narrow waist. The drive fir perfection must be contained. It can drive a human mad.

She feels her waist.

Sticks her thumbs into the grooves of her jutting hips and stares into the river.

When the cells still have the potential tae develop into other, better cell types they are called pluripotent. Sun dapples the path outtae naewhere uhn she stretches her bare legs toward it. She wills the cells to strive for perfection. She says in her mind over and over, you can do it! Don't settle for less. I'll settle for less if you promise never ever to do so, not even from day one. Her sisters are gonnae think she's a fuckin idiot! Somewhere in her throat the threat of tears present themselves as an angry persistent lump that keeps returning. She forces it back down. This year wasnae meant tae be like this.

There's No Place Like

ROSS SAYERS

Nice to be away but there's
nothing better than getting
and sleeping in your own bed.

It was bright but icy the day,
I'll be glad to come   , put the
heating on and stick my feet up.

Please don't let me have another.
I promised Eileen I'd be
in time for Strictly starting.

Right I better hang up, that's me
nearly   . Come round, I'll stick the
kettle on and we can have a blether.

Don't 'but mum' me, get yourself
    right now, mister. Otherwise I'll
collect you myself. Aye, I thought so.

They never arrived   last night. Text
this morning to say they stayed with
a mate. Had us worried, right enough.

That Judy Garland had it right. Lovely
having someone else make the bed but
there's no place like   .

And Maybe It Will Turn Out That Was Enough

KATE TOUGH

If you farmed livestock, or worked on a trawler – were someone whose livelihood was closely linked to slaughter, or maybe just a person who cared a little less – your default response would be to let nature take its course. But you're none of these, and so your default urge is to help it to live.

A few miles along the evening coastline, a handful of homes are throwing off a glow. Gulls skirt the air. Other gulls scuttle from you as you walk the sand. One scurries ahead in an arc. Smaller than the rest, feathers mottled brown not white, it has a wing opened like it's considering take-off, yet it keeps pacing, with the unfolded wing.

One task yesterday had been to deactivate Facebook and Instagram, to prevent a static existence – banal snaps being ascribed portent, haircuts and denim growing outmoded. Not for you the fate of previous pioneers; their photographic portraits lying flat in display cases to be ogled by post-industrial idlers.

You've never had a problem with causing yourself harm (junk food during a hangover, saying yes when you meant no, picking at scabs before they were ready thereby chancing your luck with a scar). For this reason you know that today will go swimmingly.

This morning, half a dozen emails were retrieved from Drafts, checked over and the delay-send function set to ten hours. Then you

97

changed the password for your email account to an arbitrary sequence of symbols and digits that you didn't note down. You signed out.

Repeatedly, recently, you've been visualising yourself succeeding, step after step: the long drive, the gullet burn, startling cold, gasp reflex. You'd assumed that was the basic principle of goal-focused psychology: an athlete achieves a personal best by mentally rehearsing the challenge and the sequential actions required to complete it.

The penny drops. It's broken. The wing is sitting open because it cannot close.

Before turning off your laptop at midday you watched a clip on YouTube showing how to wipe a hard drive. You followed the instructions. Any documents that would make matters easier over the following weeks were printed out already, sitting in poly-pockets.

The half-spent mortgage would clear itself soon, unless there was a clause in the insurance. You weren't sure if it was ever your flat or if the bank was just letting you live there. To help empty the fridge, you had lunch. Then tied the bin bag (which also contained your unwashed laundry; the decadence of that) and gave the houseplants a good drink (there was no shinjū pact with the plants).

A little over a decade from now, you would have found yourself walking home during a sunset so immense, so immersive in its rose-gold synaesthetic surround-sound, that it would've carried you into its glimmering sticky heart and you'd have buckled, momentarily, and needed the metal electricity box to support the fact of you.

The most basic mobile phone you could find in the supermarket came with a modest amount of credit. Without transferring any numbers, you'd selected 'factory settings' on your smartphone left that in the drawer, putting the primitive handset in your bag before you left, feeling unable to relinquish a phone entirely. Pulling closed the front door brought a settling sensation: now you were really heading for home.

Initial internet research had taken you sideways and offered up a theory that humans are adapted for water, because early homo sapiens had spent significant periods connected to shore environments, which explained our greasy water-resistant birthing fluids and capacity to dive for minutes at a time. Discovering this had reinforced that you were making a natural choice. You were going to a place your body would understand.

On the passenger seat, a small backpack contained a sheet of printed directions for your final destination. There was a seven-hour journey ahead and another hour, give or take, till darkness. The stereo came alive to Primal Scream.

You'd had to email, if only so they'd know where to retrieve you. What use was leaving a note (or yourself) in your home; for whom to find? A neighbour you'd swapped Christmas cards with one time, after they noticed a smell?

In your early, idle considerations, when you'd thought that deleting social media accounts might feature, you'd been inspired to go for a last root around, typing in names of people you'd never looked for before. The person you'd lost your virginity to. You'd clicked on the thumbnail that looked most like your dalliance (is that the right noun?) and landed on the Facebook page of a successful American porn actor (is that the right noun?), and had to scrutinise his photographs because, to be honest, you still couldn't quite tell (he did look more like the person you remember than the middle-aged sack of salt in Dundee sharing the name). You'd congratulated the universe on its circular sense of humour because, not long after sharing yourself sexually for the first time, you'd heard from a classmate that the man who hadn't automatically become your boyfriend after all was skipping college to shag anyone within a mile radius who was free during the day (a married woman, a single mum, a pregnant teen). A few weeks later he'd lowered his calf-like lashes and asked to borrow some money until his monthly grant came through, and you'd promptly gone to the cash machine (you had no understanding that you could cut ties with people who treated you badly, having grown up dependent upon them) then you'd never seen him again because he'd spent your money on a coach ticket.

This young one will never get the chance to use those wings. And the other gulls are not paying its plight any attention.

Efforts had long felt low on rewards. Increasingly so. Everything – day in, week out, month in, year out – was your responsibility, your decision, your task. The income, the mortgage, stocking the fridge, cooking, keeping the place clean, air in the tyres, researching the best deals on car insurance, home insurance, broadband, interest rates, gas, electricity, helping the elderly (for all the use you'd been, she'd died on you anyway), reading the meters, booking a boiler service, car service, dentist, hygienist, haircut, optician, smear, breast check, enough yet? Organising a weekend, scheduling the fun. Not that any of those demands presented impossible hardship, but they didn't exactly add up to a vision board, so why not make this decision all on your own, too? This task? Taking care of the rest.

The windscreen wipers slid intermittently to deal with spattering drizzle. Flat-headed hills dominated the windscreen, their lumpen slopes streaked with clumps of bloomless heather, looking like joints of meat just after the gravy was poured. While skipping from Primal Scream to the Cocteau Twins (yes, you'd done the solipsistic sift through your music collection for the bands most defining of your decades, to play in the car) the radio interjected. The presenter asked an interviewee, 'So, what's next for you?'

'What's next?' he said back. 'Never think about next, always just do the thing you're doing. When it's time for next you'll know.'

All well and good, but what if *next* had never arrived.

You'd developed, or maybe inherited, a sixth sense for the types who could be at risk and the types who never would be. The homes you'd visited where duvet covers had been fastened so that the buttons were hidden inside the seam (by a person not troubled by the time that method took, not wondering what the point of it was).

It was permissible, you'd observed, to talk briefly and in hazy detail about other people who might have died this way. But not to express a view that it was reasonable.

However just because previous generations had been unforgiving when their children cohabited or had children outside wedlock, or kissed someone of the same gender, it didn't mean their children shouldn't have gone ahead and exercised their rights to do so. You were breaching the fence at the final frontier.

It was almost a decade before you'd slept with anyone, after the philanderer. A shaky start could do that to a person.

You'd had to compose the emails so they'd know it wasn't a blip but rather a decision. That you hadn't entered a hormonal shitstorm of peri-menopause and succumbed to a dark place. That you weren't being bullied at work. It wasn't because you'd lost your savings playing bingo online. Wasn't because friends your age had begun developing auto-immune conditions and tumours. Wasn't because your mum's cousin had done the same thing when he'd got back from The Falklands. And wasn't because of anything you still blamed them for. It was so much simpler, like a job you hadn't enjoyed for a while – if you couldn't find enough reasons to stay, it was time to exit.

In earlier storms the bird must have been blown against something, or could the force of the wind alone break a new wing?

A well-meaning woman, your father's third wife was something of a one trick pony when it came to humour. After asking how you were, her second question was always whether you'd met a nice man yet, then answering your silence with, 'Not to worry luvvy, I'll knit you a boyfriend shall I? Ha ha ha!'

Ha ha ha. She could knit herself a step-daughter after the funeral.

Seeing him online – his puffy face, his NHS walking aid – you'd gone back and forth for a couple of days about whether to contact him, to tell him you thought he was selfish. Exploitative. An aggressor. But you hadn't – and weren't sure if that's because you didn't have the courage, or you were too embarrassed to admit what had happened. That you'd let it happen. Ashamed you'd taken part and then waited thirty-three years to mention you were bothered. That it had hurt, actually.

Or maybe you questioned what could be gained by slamming a mobility-challenged grandfather for his teenage behaviour. Whatever stopped you, you hadn't been impressed with yourself. You were able to stop thinking about it and fall asleep by telling yourself it could be a moot point soon, if you wished.

You'd cross-referenced online maps with your road atlas, noting where to leave the car, where to find the path, where the sand changed to rocks. Into your small pack you'd put two litres of vodka and ankle weights from the sports shop. Plus a head-torch, because if you ended up parking the car in darkness you wouldn't be sitting it out until first light.

The mammalian dive reflex could be honed; the body trained to stay underwater for several minutes, with a much slowed heartbeat and reduced rate of oxygen conversion. Purposely, you had not practiced in the bath. You'd be relying on your non-honed responses and the keen rate of your pulse, which was familiar from the nights when you'd lain on your stomach waiting for sleep, ear pressed into the pillow, hearing your heart coming back at you, magnified within the trembling tunnels of the mattress springs.

You began to need to pee. You laughed, realising you could soak yourself, soak your seat, because surely now there were no rules. But it would make the rest of the day uncomfortable and besides, it was hardly a Bucket List top ten – wetting yourself. You held it, played chicken with your bladder to add edge to your last car journey. You watched for the next sign for services and pondered why you hadn't made a Bucket List. What *were* the things you'd always wanted to try? Had that contributed to this; forgetting to try new things? Forgetting to want to?

Twelve years hence, a child you would have been related to would've shared his explanation for why squirrels don't have to go to school every day, like he did, and you'd have welled up for a second or two, thinking of him with no one to tell.

You wanted only enough lung capacity not to panic, and to cover enough distance that a return swim would be impossible.

You imagined the final intake of breath. You'd been imagining it often. A reflexive draw inward. The sensation as the air begs to be released. Empty lungs refilling with something as unsuited as water. You imagined the agony for as long as you could.

Most cars had lights on for the gloomy conditions. You registered a set of headlights dead on, in the near distance. Growing closer. Attempting a *double* overtake? There wouldn't be time. The temptation was strong to face-off with that idiot – not to make your death look like an accident, too late for that with the emails set to detonate – because if you let the car collide with yours, wouldn't *that* show the driver. People couldn't be let off the hook their whole lives. How would they learn? They were in the wrong lane, let them deal with the consequences. You were Thelma (or Louise; you forget which).

The front vehicle being overtaken braked sharply, as did you, to enable the over-taker to weave back into lane with a second to spare. Everyone took responsibility for the stupidity to make sure no one died. In the nano-second that your car passed his, you flicked two-fingers and tried to eyeball him but he employed the tactic of looking straight ahead to avoid admission of guilt or chance of remonstration.

Your behaviour was depressing – point-scoring on driving skills through glass. *Get a life*, you told yourself, smirking.

It was reasonable to expect you'd spend a journey such as this doing a reckoning, an inventory of how well you'd conducted yourself and whether there were loose ends. But no need. Everything that was ever expected of you, you'd fulfilled. You had not been letting yourself or anyone else down. Your life was far from a TV mini-series.

Coach tour season was in full June force and the services were awash with grey heads. You felt decades younger than those people but doing the arithmetic proved you were not. You joined the queue for the loos, and afterwards paused as you were leaving. It hadn't occurred to you that you'd need another meal but the plan would only happen if you had the energy to complete it.

You'd have to eat there rather than pick up a snack because eating while driving was illegal and wouldn't that put a dampener on things, to be pulled over for holding half a sandwich, and then fail to present yourself and your driving licence at a police station within the required seven days, thus becoming a posthumous criminal. Which the local paper would upscale: **Tragic Beach Woman Running From Police.**

As you'd emerged from sleep some weeks ago it dawned, for the first time, that back passage penetration didn't count as loss of virginity. Not that he'd mentioned anything, so you thought he was making a mistake in the darkness, which he'd correct at any moment. You hadn't wanted to embarrass him by pointing out his lack of basic knowledge. You hadn't known you could speak during sex because you had no experience of sex. Or of speaking up generally. Or of how uncomfortable it would be for days afterwards.

Have gulls no strategy for mending their own? What are this wee thing's chances?

Walking towards the exit you passed a long cabinet of refrigerated drinks and wondered whether you should grab a bottle of water for the remaining hours. So you did.

You didn't screech out of the car-park like the bandit you were but you checked your rear-view mirror a few times. You were a common thief and you'd have to live with that for the rest of your life (figures of speech have acquired an amusing dimension).

Back in the flow of single file traffic, you didn't want to start getting sentimental but it showed up anyway – you'd eaten your ultimate meal. Shuffling along the cafeteria queue you hadn't been thinking LAST SUPPER, hadn't piled calorific treats onto your tray, just leek-and-potato soup, carried to the nearest seat, and the person who'd served you had forgotten your ration of butter.

You had your reasons why fifty-one years were sufficient, and that had been the gist of the emails: *Don't torment yourselves with what you could have done differently, this is not an escape from something specific or an ending of anguish, it's what I'm choosing, and the prospect gives me great peace, so this is not an apology either. Thank you for the good times* (careful not to spell those out, better to let them think that there were some) *and for not dwelling on this.*

Other people's experience of being alive must feel to them like they're torches lined up, ablaze along the ramparts. It must because otherwise, why would they hang about? (Though you'd walked past new-build blocks with cat climbing-frames blocking the front glass and flat-screen slabs screwed to the walls, and suspected that maybe, it did not.)

Your father's third wife (whose name you've never managed to retain) always insisted on her Christmas Day tradition (if two years counted as a tradition) of 'couples photos' – her with your dad, your brothers with their wives, your niece with her girlfriend – inevitably spending several minutes after everyone else had drifted away trying to get the dog to sit still, for you to have your picture taken.

So many degrees of separation stood between that living room, that grouping, and the house you'd grown up in; you could never understand why you were there.

It was nearly three decades before comments in the online environment had educated you that plenty of men liked to enter a woman's body by her rectum and that *of course* he'd known what he was doing. Had felt entitled to without consultation.

And you hadn't been able to look after yourself in your own room; suggesting that you lacked the skills which others possess to cultivate a haven.

Trees thinned out along the roadside to reveal a high half-hexagon footbridge over rail tracks, and a white-painted station house, and a few hundred yards further along you caught up with three moving carriages which had recently left the station. You kept pace with the train, lit from the inside, occupied in sets of two seats or four, travellers, people lost in phone screens, all of whom would be gone within a hundred years. Some within five. A few sooner than that.

Nobody was ending up anywhere but dead.

And it wasn't anyone's job to search for you, public services were underfunded enough without being a drain. So in four hours they'd know where you were, if they picked up email notifications at 9 p.m. on weekends.

Forest resumed at road level. Hulking mountain outlines in shades of coal and graphite sat like jurors. A lick of light, blue-ish white, cut into the dusk. A quarter-mile later another flash inside low cloud—whap! Like something was wanting through, something trying to force a hole in the fabric. And the brutal wind could rip the rest, so a torn sheaf of sky and hill would spill over on itself, like the visible world was a painted backdrop and the scenery would be hanging half-off, to reveal—

You'd remembered someone mentioning that Facebook had a hidden messages function, a second mailbox you hadn't known about, and as soon as you could you'd located it and checked.

Nothing was waiting. There was no parallel life where surprise mails arrived with thrilling content. If you were honest, you'd sort of known that before you'd looked.

It came down in torrents and the traffic slowed to thirty. Sloshes of water rose to window level as you coursed the sloping camber. Inevitable, maybe, that the journey would go like this. Biblically raging and thrashing. Testing your resolve to carry on.

This baby gull is not your problem. Absolutely. Is not yours. You have no veterinary knowledge. You have plans.

An onset of hailstones engulfed you in white noise, save for the thump of wipers on hyper mode. In June. *It won't work, God mate.*

You'd lain there a few weeks back, as the light began to creep around the curtains, not knowing whether to be more upset by the fact you'd basically paid a guy who'd violated you, or that you were a virgin till you were 27.

On Facebook you'd seen his adult daughter and hoped she'd never met a teen help-himself-er like her dad.

That you were useful wasn't in doubt. Dare you say liked, too. But a person could be useful and liked on a Residents' Association committee and still not want to be on the Residents' Association committee. Not being able to enjoy a hen weekend didn't mean you were depressed, it just meant you didn't see any reason for hen weekends.

Beyond the turn-off for the last sizeable town the road became quieter, narrowed to single width in some stretches. You passed access tracks to farms and occasional rows of old cottages, between long stretches of no human evidence.

You spent the miles testing whether it was possible to push empty space around your skull, through the brain's compact, curling folds.

Waiting at the bus stop after college, one of them had spoken up from within the huddle of boy-men scuffling past, 'Lorna likes it up the arse!'

It was days before you'd twigged that it wasn't a non-sequitur. And where they'd got their intel from. *Not by choice she doesn't!* you would scream at them, if you had a TARDIS.

Who got to decide how many years were enough years? There wasn't a proscribed length – the time a life lasted was the length of it and you had done as much as you were prepared to.

It relaxed you, knowing that you weren't obliged have any further part in it.

The light had fallen by another lumen or two.

As listed on your printout, there was a wide verge with space for several cars. You parked and hesitated by the door with your key in your hand, wondering whether to take it with you. How would that help? You decided to treat it like a hired car and tucked the key behind a tyre.

A grassy path ended at the beach where a heavy breeze was moving wisps of fore-cloud at a clip past weightier back-cloud.

It was a relief to be there. Arriving on the sand was like walking down the aeroplane steps at the start of a holiday, anticipating the liberated bliss.

One night near your sixtieth birthday your phone would have rung at 1.47am and the twenty-year-old daughter of a friend (who'd died of an aneurysm the previous year) would be barely be able to articulate why she was crying. You'd have done your best to calm her and asked if she was in immediate danger. You'd have told her to find the nearest street sign, asked if she could see a 24-hour shop or petrol station and kept her on speaker-phone as you'd dressed. And you'd have said *sorry sorry sorry sorry* to your fifty-one-year-old self, your eighteen-year-old self, as you'd driven through the street-lit city to reach her.

It's tugging on you – the knowledge that there's a chance it could live if someone who knew about these things could attend to it. But who would ever know if you phoned for help or if you didn't? Your conscience will run out in twenty minutes. You do not have to care about this.

Hobbling with its broken limb. It knows something is hurting. It doesn't know why. You can watch its pain but you cannot watch its inability to take care of the pain.

Like the saucepan seen on the hob after you think you've finished washing the dishes, it appears that your duties aren't quite done. With the pay-as-you-go mobile you call an inquiry service that you'd never normally use because it releases phone numbers for extortionate sums. There's a fleeting curiosity – if you'd lived like this more often, taken trips, spent money like there were no consequences, would you be having a life you currently didn't wish to leave? But answering that is like attempting to go back through a valve.

When you give the animal charity call-handler the bird's location, she asks if she can pass your number to the regional officer on duty out-of-hours. This feels in conflict with the digital disconnection you've spent the past couple of days taking care of. What are you going to do, refuse?

A little after hanging up, your phone rings. The guy recaps the information you'd given to the operator. He asks you, 'Is there a towel you can put over it?"

You didn't pack a towel. You hadn't planned on getting back out. 'Wouldn't it waddle around, dragging a towel?' you reply.

'Once the towel's over it you can pick it up.'

'Why would I pick it up?' The thought of a struggling bird beneath cloth is abhorrent.

'Take it to your house and I'll collect it.'

'I'm not staying anywhere I'm… on holiday.'

'Is there a box you can put over it and a stone on the box, so I'll see it when I get there?'

'I'd have to look along the beach. Won't it be stressed, trapped under a box?'

'Right enough, I'll bring a seabird therapist with me, how's that?' But he speaks before you have time to. 'It's an hour for me to get there. It would help to know it's secure.'

This is someone's Saturday night you're spoiling. Piss or get off the pot, woman, do the man a favour. 'I'll see what I can find and call you back.'

'If you can, love, the sooner the better, it's getting dark.'

You find a washed up creel but it's too small and has latticed rope on all sides. Wandering further you find a broken wooden crate and pick it up.

You'd lifted out your tent pegs, one by one, and here you are. *Involved.*

A new thing you find out about yourself in your twilight is that you can run faster than an injured young gull. The hurt wing has to be tucked forcibly within the confines of the box and the anguish this causes you both is considerable. You run to the tide line to rinse your fingers of lice that you're sure must be on them.

Shaking water from your hands you're reminded of something you'd read online, about the portion of sea between shore and horizon being known as the offing. Which means your death is literally in the offing.

You reach for the phone to call the officer back and notice the time. So. Your emails have hit. For thirteen minutes people have been party to your decision. Except you'd been aiming for the poetry of them reading the messages while you were committing the act. But as noted, your life isn't a split-screen mini-series.

You return to the road behind the beach to call him with less wind blasting into the mouthpiece. You tell him about the box and the rock.

He's thanking you from a speakerphone, adding, 'I've put the beach into my GPS. It's a pretty remote spot you've found for yourself. At this time of night. You lost?'

'No. Was going for a swim. I'm an enthusiast…of wild swimming. At night.'

'A keen swimmer. With no towel.'

You have no answer.

'I'm not sure it's the weather for it. You got someone with you?'

'Uh, I left details at the guest house. I probably won't now, like you say, it's rougher than I'd realised. You know what it's like on holiday, spontaneous ideas. There'll be another beach tomorrow, I'm up here for a week, so…'

'Tomorrow sounds more sensible. Better yet, a flight to Greece. Anyway, the quicker I get there, the quicker I get home. Happy days. You take care, angel.'

After he disconnects you hear the silence. Facing back to the sea there's a deep turquoise swatch where light squeezing through black cloud is landing on choppy crests.

In an hour he'll be at your beach.

Calling you angel.

Maybe you could go on a campaign to injure creatures so you can keep phoning him. Maybe there's a sheep you could kick.

The sea is starting to look like it's being absorbed by the sky; there's barely any light.

And your family and friends know. And what would the next decades be like living alongside these people whose first thought every time they saw you would be, 'Is she plotting again?' Scanning your eyes for signs.

You ponder whether there will be long-adapted amphibious humans waiting for you. Under-sea nomads to take you in.

You know, though, that you cannot risk being at the beach when he arrives. And you don't have time to find another beach. It's close to pitch black.

You do not need the sea. You have the vodka.

A man on YouTube had died on a dancefloor, after he was filmed downing a bottle of tequila for a dare. So two bottles of vodka should be ample.

There's an opening in the dyke where a gate came off its hinges and wasn't replaced. You turn the car into the field, trundle over the uneven ground and tuck in, close to the wall. Enough to be invisible tonight, though not in the morning.

There's a sliver of yellow northern night, sitting along the horizon, below the storm clouds.

You're typing out a text to leave displayed on your screen. An apology to whomever happens to find you. Battery charge lasts for days in these phones.

You screw the top off the first litre and begin to gulp, as steadily as you can, given the corrosive slick of every swallow. With each slant of the cold bottle you're imagining the nightclub crowd, with bets placed, cheering and chanting you on.

Roots

ANDRÉS N. ORDORICA

What's left of mis raíces
when the flower has been plucked
plunged deeply into water?

Does the flower still count
if it's only stem and petal
and is dying in the vase?

What's left of mis raíces
when the dirt that bore me
is blown away by a storm?

Or as the well runs dry
and the earth cracks open
angry and all consuming?

If the roots have withered
can I still blossom
am I still allowed to grow?

What's left of mis raíces
if in the land of my ancestors
my family is no more?

HH

THOMAS McCABE

You can stay until you get sorted,
you said. I buried my head.
A promise: the oasis, a den to rest, shelter,
maybe still alone, but no longer out there with the hyenas.
Trust you, trust me,
trust in *you can stay until you get sorted.*

Proper shipwrecked, gnawed at,
I saw it coming, like creeping city-centre construction.
'Coalition government', bad decisions, only human, redundant,
canvas incoming. So I thought:
A noble defeat. But it's not.
Last straw is just salt. Still,
there's a rest on the canvas.
I have somewhere to stay
until I get sorted.

Six hours on the floor
and the geese are flying.
One storm to another: a leash of shifting foxes,
life in stop-motion, a staggered eclipse, six minutes standing up.

I guess that's how storms work... when they arrive
it's already too late. My wee girl, only five,
taken from my arms at seven thirty, my three-year-old a bemused spectator.
So much shouting, but I can't make out what's being said.
Tears, but not from me,
a blizzard, snowblind.

Now transported to a new oasis,
6 feet tall atop a hill, bathing in sunrise, scanning city rooftops.
A new kingdom: memories of Spain,
a world away (have pulse? alive?).
Skin is warm, thankful for small victories.
So, this is me now,
parent, redundant, homeless.

Best get myself sorted.

My alarm call for school was sounding. 'Vehicle reversing, vehicle reversing.' It was very early, but I had a lot to do. I made my way to the train station where, for a couple of pounds, I had access to the toilets and a locker with clean clothes. I was still cold and numb when I walked past the lorries being unloaded into the back of the Princes Street shops. The street cleaners sang as they worked. I wondered if they could tell that I'd spent the night in the car park, but my attention soon focused as I arrived at the bright lights and commuters of the station. A quick wash in warm water and a set of clean clothes made me feel so much better, and I managed to get to registration class on time. I wasn't sure how much longer I could keep this up.

School was great and provided some normality and routine, although I was tired and found myself getting frustrated by my friends and peers. Not having the tickets for the concert, the latest trainers or a top to match their outfit for the weekend might have been their biggest problem. I found myself feigning interest and sympathy as I became more and more distant from them. I knew that it wasn't their fault, but it didn't stop me feeling like screaming. Each class was an escape, stopped me thinking about what was going to happen next. At the end of the day, when everyone started making plans to meet up, I made my excuses and headed back into the city centre.

My locker at the station had enough layers to get me through the night but I was running low on clean clothes. As it began to get dark, I headed for my pitch, a doorway on the North Bridge, and I put a little of the change I had left in the bottom of a polystyrene cup to stop it from blowing away. The pavement was cold, I needed to find some more cardboard to sit on and a blanket to wrap around my legs. I shouted across to Adam on the other side of the road to see if he had anything I could use. It was funny how quickly I had become friends with the street community. At first everyone had tried to encourage me to return home, but when they realised I wasn't going to do that they began to look out for me, ensuring that I had someone nearby whenever I sat down for the night. These friends had kept me safe and given me food and clothes before I realised that the only way to survive was to make money for myself.

With extra cardboard and a blanket, I sat down for the night, hoping that I would get a decent drop and not have to stay out long. I kept my hood up, not just because it was cold, but because I really didn't want to get caught by anyone who knew me or might report me. I watched the world go by: it was almost like those timelapse videos you see on the television, as folk go rushing past to get home from work or meet friends for dinner. I'd never felt quite as invisible as I did sitting there. Occasionally when people stopped to drop some coins in the cup, I got to look them in the face and say thank you, but otherwise it was like I didn't exist. I had learned quickly to take the money out of the cup and keep it fairly empty – there were people willing to rob and hurt you to get that cash. Each time someone stopped, I took some of the coins out and put them in a pocket or a shoe, ensuring that if I was approached I could empty one pocket and pretend that what I was giving them was all that I had.

After raising enough money for a chippy for dinner, lunch the next day and a trip to the launderette, I called it a night, heading back to Rose Street to my skipper. The car park was quiet late at night, except for the humming of the ventilation which blew out some warm air and the occasional drunken wanderer looking for a quiet corner to relieve themselves. I had been advised that it was best to find somewhere sheltered, somewhere I wouldn't be seen by the public and potential predators, but would also be heard if I needed to scream for help. This car park was the perfect spot. I hoped that I would get a couple of hours sleep undisturbed between the pubs closing and the deliveries of tomorrow arriving. Wriggling down into my sleeping bag, I could feel the cold ground even through the two layers of cardboard beneath me. The night was going to be hard, and I knew with winter fast approaching it was going to get colder yet.

As if the cold wasn't bad enough, my busy brain was keeping me awake now, trying to make plans for the following day. I wondered how I could get my washing done and make it to school. Maybe I just had to give that up for now and focus on finding a better place to stay for the winter. Maybe, I thought, I need to tell people what is happening and get some help, but I had tried that before and they left me at home. In this car park, in the doorway and on the streets, there was a risk I would get hurt, but at home there was a certainty. I knew if I just kept going I could make it until I was 16 and I would be an adult, able to get indoors and get some help. It wasn't long now and I had made it this far.

'Bleep, bleep, bleep, vehicle reversing, vehicle reversing.' It couldn't really have been morning again already. There was no way I was getting to school. I was going to go to the pool and get a proper shower and spend the day in the launderette. First, I would use my cash to get clean clothes from the charity shop so that I could get everything washed, and then I could maybe sit for a while to get some more cash to eat later. Decision made. I knew that there was a risk that the school would call home, that he would have to tell them I wasn't living there. I would be reported missing and would have to hide from the police more than ever. That was a problem for another day though, all that mattered now were clean clothes and enough money to eat.

I never returned to school. Scared that I would be caught and taken home, I just kept moving, and soon enough, one day blurred into the next. I could see how people got stuck in this routine, of making money to survive, finding a place to sleep and keep warm, supporting one another. However, watching people inject themselves to escape what they were feeling and how they were living, having a gun pointed at my head for the change in my cup, having coins thrown at my head by passers-by who told me to get a job, and, of course, the (all too generous) offers of a place to stay for the night by lonely older men was all too much. I needed to get out.

I had been 16 for a while and had been offered a place in a hostel, but even walking past it was intimidating and I didn't want to live with all the adults I'd seen on the streets. Instead, I asked a youth worker I had known for a while if they could help me sort out a house, and I began, with their support, to navigate my way through the benefits and housing systems. I was quickly able to get keys for a flat in an undesirable part of town. While it was still secured with a steel door and windows which would be removed prior to my official move in date, I didn't care, I took my sleeping bag and moved in. It had no lightbulbs, carpets, curtains, but even the bare floorboards and a little candle were homely enough, and I had a door that I could lock. Being able to sleep without one eye open was everything. I slept well on my first night and better with every night that followed as I got used to the noise, or lack of it. My youth worker helped me to find furniture and make the house a home and in no time at all I was able to manage my bills and keep myself fed. I started a wee job in a café and applied for college. I really wanted to finish my Highers so that I could eventually be a youth worker for someone else. I had found a house and had been able to make it a home and was compelled now to ensure that everyone else who was facing homelessness could get out and find a way home for themselves.

Now, as an adult, people often ask me if I would do it all again. I tell them that I do it every day: I jump out of windows, find friends and supporters, look for a safe skipper and chase the money to keep going. If I have learned anything from my journey it is the importance of resilience and determination, and while I long for a day when we can stop, when young people are kept safe and no longer have to experience homelessness, until then we will keep working to end youth homelessness forever.

About Rock Trust

Rock Trust is Scotland's only youth homelessness charity.

Early in 1990, it was discovered that homeless young people had been sleeping rough in the graveyard of St Cuthbert's Church, Edinburgh. The Council of West End Churches (St Cuthbert's, St John's and St Andrew's and St George's) was shocked by this harsh reality, and moved to action. The Council at the time owned a flat occupied by friars, members of the Society of St Francis. One of them, Brother Basil, set out to publicise the issue of youth homelessness and raise funds. His energy turned an ambition into reality, and in 1991 Rock Trust was formed.

In 1991, the objectives of Rock Trust were to provide educational materials, to do something practical, to provide easy access to advice and support services, education on benefits income, and a safe place for young people to go. In terms of their objectives, little has changed since 1991, but their means to fulfil them has. In February 1993, as a direct consequence of an anonymous donation of £100,000, a flat was opened for homeless young people, with three more opening later in the year. This was a ground-breaking moment in the development of the charity, forming the Bedrock service which still operates today.

In 2002, Rock Trust moved to 55 Albany Street, where they are still based today. For 30 years they have been striving to support young people who are dealing with homelessness, and to shine a light on both the visible and invisible realities of homelessness. The services they offer young people have been developed to address the broad range of needs and experiences of young people, with an emphasis on creating choice. No one version of support is appropriate for every person. That is why their services range from long-term support for young people with very complex needs, such as those leaving care, to emergency support for young people in crisis, to a helping hand for young people who are simply struggling to access an expensive and competitive rental market.

In addition to accommodation, they help their young people to progress in their lives so that they can overcome personal barriers and move on from homelessness for good. Rock Trust has always believed that homelessness is more than rooflessness and that young people need to learn social and practical skills to be active participating members of their community and society.

The young people they work with have access to a variety of opportunities to learn and develop, depending on where they are in their lives. Rock Trust can provide 1–1 support workers, mentors, mediation, and health and wellbeing support, alongside regular evening groups such as a cooking club, employability drop-in and short educational courses. In this way they can ensure that the most vulnerable young people in our society can avoid or move on from homelessness for good, and have the futures they deserve.

Maida Gibson (left), a former Rock Trust Board member and Brother Basil (right), now Father Basil. A former Anglican Franciscan, Father Basil was the founding director of Rock Trust.

Left to right: Bob Stewart, first staff appointment and Project Worker with the Bedrock Project. Appointed in 1992, he had worked with SACRO (Scottish Association for the Care and Resettlement of Offenders) and been employed for many years by the Cyrenians; Ruth Innes, Communications Officer for Rock Trust, organised the first National Sleep Out in Edinburgh at the end of 1993; Bill Clarke, Project Worker.

A group of people set off around Edinburgh on Rock Trust's first ever
Sponsored Cycle.